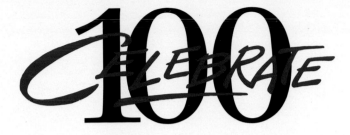

THE WASHINGTON STATE CENTENNIAL COOKBOOK

ROMAR BOOKS, LTD.
Seattle, Washington

Celebrate 100: The Washington Centennial Cookbook
Copyright © 1989 by Romar Books, Ltd.

Published by Romar Books, Ltd.
18002 15th Ave. NE, Suite B
Seattle, Washington 98155-3838

First Edition

Printed and bound in the United States of America.

ISBN 0-945265-05-0

Library of Congress Catalog Card Number 89-091050

Photography by Barry Gregg
Cover and book design by Lee Wallat and Peggy Young

TABLE OF CONTENTS

TABLE OF CONTENTS (CONTINUED)

Food and Cooking Terms for *Celebrate 100*

baste: to keep food moist and add flavor while cooking, usually by spooning melted fat, pan juice, wine or other liquid over the surface.

blanche: to plunge into boiling water for the purpose of softening a food, or for partial precooking.

brown: to turn the surface of food brown in color by cooking quickly in hot fat on top of the stove or at a high temperature in the oven or broiler.

chinois: a conical strainer.

clarified butter (to prepare): cut sticks of butter into half-inch slices and melt over low heat. Skim off foam; then spoon the clarified butter (the clear liquid under the foam) into another container and discard the milky residue that has settled at bottom of pan.

crème fraîche: combination of 1 part sour cream and 2 parts whipping cream, heated to 110 degrees and left at room temperature until thick, about 8 hours.

deep-fry: to cook food by immersing in hot fat or oil.

deglaze: to collect the concentrated cooking juices remaining in the pan after sautéing or roasting food, by adding a small amount of liquid to the pan and scraping the browned particles and meat juices into the liquid as it cooks, thus dissolving them.

dice: to cut into very small, even cubes.

julienne: to cut into thin, match-like strips.

mirepoix: a preparation of diced vegetables most often used to enhance the flavor of meat, but also used in the preparation of sauces and as a garnish for some dishes.

nap: to cover food with a sauce.

poach: to cook food by immersing in a liquid that is barely simmering.

reduce: to boil a liquid rapidly, reducing its quantity by evaporation and thus concentrating and intensifying its flavor.

roux: a mixture of equal parts butter and flour, blended over low heat and used as a thickening agent.

sauté: to cook food in a small amount of hot fat.

simmer: to cook a liquid barely at the boiling point. The surface should show only a few bubbles breaking slowly.

steam: to cook by means of vapor rising through the food from boiling liquid.

stock: the seasoned liquid in which meat, fish, poultry or vegetables have been cooked.

STATE OF WASHINGTON
OFFICE OF THE GOVERNOR

OLYMPIA
98504-0413

BOOTH GARDNER
GOVERNOR

Dear Reader,

Birthdays and good eating go hand in hand. A cookbook in celebration of Washington's Centennial is a most fitting tribute.

All of the senses should be involved in celebrating Washington's Centennial, including taste. The recipes of this cookbook come from the chefs of Washington's finest restaurants and were carefully selected to mirror the state's rich cultural diversity to make this experience in taste a most enjoyable adventure.

The state's 100th Birthday is a time of reflection and renewal. It is a "feast," if you will, of past, present, and future. Books like this will help to make the next 100 years as good or better than the last.

Sincerely,

Booth Gardner
Governor

Dear Friends around the table and around the world,

We are delighted to invite you to join in the celebration of Washington's 100 years, by cooking, tasting, and sharing these favorite recipes from many of the state's best cooks — from the menus of their restaurants as well as their own home kitchens.

Peace Table is a project in International Culinary Diplomacy created to allow people of all countries and ethnic backgrounds to share simple, yet important moments in the growing, gathering, cooking and tasting of our traditional foods. We feel strongly that food truly is the common bond among the peoples of the world, and that by cooking in each other's kitchens and experiencing the culinary heritage of our respective countries we can celebrate and savor our similarities, thus opening new pathways of communication and understanding.

Gathering around the table, making and breaking bread together is one of the oldest rituals known to people, harvesting the fruits of the earth for the sustenance of body and soul. We are now rediscovering the importance of returning to our roots as the natural step in creating harmony among all people and stewardship for the future of Mother Earth.

Peace Table encourages international cultural exchange visits among cooks, bakers, restaurant and cafe workers, market farmers, and cooking students. This is people to people diplomacy.

Therefore, it is important to introduce the people of Washington State who have dedicated their life's work to the preservation and enhancement of our region's bounty of edible treasures. The culinary traditions of this area have evolved from the Northwest

Peace Table 9792 Edmonds, WA 98020 (206) 546-6816

Indians who lived close to the land and survived by foraging for wild roots and berries and by harvesting native salmon, to the pioneer homesteaders who ploughed the first furrows for the planting and harvesting of the first crops. The tradition continued with the farm families of yesterday and today. Their lives reflect this same closeness to the land and their lifestyle is mirrored through the simple farmhouses they have created.

Because of the diversity and abundance of its food resources, Washington State has become an international culinary crossroads, drawing people from all over the world to savor, taste, and explore the richness and beauty of its regions. Through these experiences they discover the extraordinary warmth and friendliness which has become the spirit of our state.

It is this convivial spirit mingled with our passion for food and friendship which has led us to begin planting diplomatic seed with our culinary friends around the world.

David Chakava, a "phisicist" (his spelling) from the Peoples Friendship University in Moscow, USSR recently wrote us a letter after hearing a Peace Table interview, featuring five prominent Seattle chefs on Radio Moscow. Here are the highlights of his letter!

To get closer by means of cooking together! An excellent and very profound idea, showing that universal goals can be achieved by simple and ordinary means, if there is a desire and goodwill.

I wouldn't believe that (I) could influence somehow the policy making. I am a phisicist and have nothing to do with cooking (except when I'm hungry). But I'm ready to put on a cooker's cap if it will help me find new friends in America.

Ordinary people, who really do have much in common, no matter where they live in the US and USSR, elsewhere, will come to terms much quicker than politicians and thus contributing to the cause of Peace.

We dedicate the Washington Centennial Cookbook to this spirit of culinary diplomacy... that the language of food transcends boundaries, borders, and political differences and allows everyday people the opportunity to build lasting bridges to international understanding. From a simple farmhouse supper in the Snohomish Valley to a resplendent Soviet Georgian feast, from Seattle's historic Pike Place Market to the colorful, exciting open markets in Tashkent, Uzbekistan, the message is the same as the one that Arthur Stepanyen proclaimed in Moscow October 30, 1986:

Around the table we are all one family.

Our dream is to leave this world a better place, a more peaceful place for our children. We invite you to gather with us, around the Peace Table.

Jerilyn Brusseau

A Gourmet's Notebook

P.O. Box 12171
Seattle, WA 98112

It used to be, the family went out for Sunday dinner and dove into fried chicken or splurged on veal cutlets. The very best restaurants were steakhouses. And that was not such a long sleepy time ago.

Then a wonderful thing happened. The Northwest discovered France. And Greece and Portugal and Holland. And, more recently, Maryland soft shelled crabs and New Orleans étouffée. And most recently of all, we have discovered ourselves. We have learned to make use of the bounty of the Northwest in a cuisine truly our own.

Dining out now, in the state of Washington, is like touring the world. It was therefore a delightful assignment to be asked to select one hundred of the best restaurants in Washington. We did not assemble the one hundred biggest, nor most expensive, nor most well known. We selected the best.

Many of the restaurants are small, independently and locally owned. They have another thing in common. They serve wonderful food. Some of it is fancy, but much of it is simple. Some have invested in formal decor, while a few have none at all. In most the owner will be present.

The restaurants represent a broad variety of food styles, from the piquant, sometimes fiery food of the East to the classics of France, from juicy Southern fried chicken to pungent curries from Thailand. We now distinguish between Neopolitan and Bolognese and between Szechuan and Hunan cuisine. Crabcakes have become menu fixtures where not so long ago veal Oscar was considered exotic.

What was a solitary color not too long ago has become a culinary rainbow. Dining out Washington style is a world tour adventure.

Welcome! Enjoy!

7

PUBLISHER'S PREFACE

Celebrate 100: The Washington Centennial Cookbook has truly been a cooperative effort between the publisher and the one hundred restaurants represented in the pages of this book. Each restaurant in this cookbook has made a significant time and financial commitment to help *Celebrate 100* become a reality. The restaurants were asked to share their most cherished possessions—their recipes. For many, translating their creative and magical skills into written recipes was a difficult and time-consuming task. Arrangements also had to be made for preparation of the recipes and photography sessions. Of course, as a publisher, we wanted everything completed yesterday. A very special thanks to all the owners and chefs of the restaurants in *Celebrate 100*.

The spirit of cooperation needed to make this centennial edition a success, however, has involved many others. To ensure that *Celebrate 100: The Washington Centennial Cookbook* featured only those restaurants that are worthy of such a publication, we solicited the help of the editors of *A Gourmet's Notebook* on the basis of their reputation for being the most knowledgeable, respected, and independent food critics in the state. They have been most helpful in providing us with the names of restaurants that have a reputation for excellence among the restaurants of Washington State. We thank them for helping us make *Celebrate 100* a "world tour adventure" of 100 of Washington's finest restaurants.

To produce a quality cookbook requires the professional services and expertise of a variety of individuals. We feel that we have had the best available. The photography by Barry Gregg and the recipe preparation by food stylist Phyllis Bogard have turned each recipe into an art form. Joanne Choi's careful recipe testing has ensured the accuracy and clarity of each recipe. And the outstanding work by graphic designers Lee Wallat and Peggy Young has given *Celebrate 100* an artistic unity and quality that one would expect in a centennial publication. We deeply appreciate the fine professional work done by all these exceptionally gifted people.

To take the idea of a centennial cookbook and see it through to its becoming a finished product requires a certain kind of vision and leadership. Elizabeth Burbank had that vision and communicated it very effectively to others. Her enthusiastic commitment and organizational skills have played a significant role in making *Celebrate 100* a reality. She is to be commended for a job well done.

One of the people who also caught the vision of a centennial cookbook to celebrate Washington State's one hundredth birthday is Warren Talbott of Dayton, Washington. His backing and support of *Celebrate 100* helped make this project possible. We thank him for his involvement and are pleased that his town is represented in this cookbook.

We would be remiss if we implied that the number of fine restaurants in the state of Washington is limited to the one hundred restaurants featured in these pages. Quality is encouraged by quality. Many of Washington's restaurants have achieved their reputations of excellence by being in good company. And so our thanks to all those restaurants that have contributed to Washington State's fame for fine cuisine. To you we dedicate *Celebrate 100: The Washington Centennial Cookbook*.

CAFE SPORT
SEATTLE
GEODUCK WITH CHINESE SAUSAGE AND BLACK BEANS

2 tablespoons olive oil
2 tablespoons peanut oil
16 oz. cleaned and sliced geoduck (sliced as thin as possible)
4 oz. Chinese sausage, thinly sliced
2 teaspoons chopped garlic
2 tablespoons salted black beans (rinsed)
2 teaspoons julienned fresh ginger
1 teaspoon crushed red chilies
4 wedges of lemon
2 teaspoons soy sauce
2 teaspoons rice vinegar
8 oz. chicken stock
8 oz. cooked Chinese noodles (fried crisp)*
2 tablespoons butter
4 tablespoons cilantro, coarsely chopped

Heat oils to almost smoking in a 10-inch sauté pan. Add geoduck, sausage, garlic, beans, ginger and chilies, and sauté for one-half minute, constantly tossing and stirring around. Squeeze in juice from lemon wedges and add rinds. Add soy sauce, rice vinegar and chicken stock. After one and a half minutes or until cooked medium-rare, remove geoduck and place on fried noodles. (Do not overcook geoduck.) Reduce remaining liquid to sauce and stir in butter. Pour over geoduck and noodles. Garnish with coarsely chopped cilantro or whole cilantro leaves. Serve immediately.

* Cook noodles for 5 minutes; drain and toss in a little oil. Deep-fry until crisp; or pan fry in a lightly oiled, non-stick skillet, shaping the noodles into a 'pancake' which is then browned on both sides.

Serves 4.

Cafe Sport just celebrated its fifth anniversary at the north end of the Pike Place Market. The emphasis is on new American and Pacific Rim cuisines, with a daily changing menu. Two of the favorites at one of Seattle's most acclaimed restaurants are Black Bean Soup and Dungeness Crabcakes. Chef-manager Tom Douglas, the genial genius behind the Sport's success, is leaving on sabbatical "to rekindle the creative fires" and, to the delight of loyal patrons, will be succeeded by Seattle native Diane Isaiou, who has been with him for two years.

CREDIT CARDS: V, MC, AE, CB, DC; WHEELCHAIR ACCESS; SMOKING/NON-SMOKING; FULL BAR; RESERVATIONS ACCEPTED

2020 Western Avenue • (206) 443-6000

DOMINIQUE'S PLACE

SEATTLE

LINGUINE WITH CROQUETTES OF RABBIT

Meat:

1 deboned rabbit (leg, shoulders, loins)
½ onion
1 oz. sorrel
1 oz. parsley
2 cloves garlic, finely grated

salt, pepper
2 eggs
1 tablespoon flour
½ cup crushed pistachios

Sauce:

2 small tomatoes, seeded and "mondees,"*cut in ½-inch cubes
½ cup julienne of carrot, zucchini and leeks
1 tablespoon chopped fresh ginger
2 tablespoons composed butter (mixture of butter, fresh herbs such as basil, parsley, spinach, sorrel, cress or fennel, almonds, walnuts, lemon juice and garlic)

1 teaspoon lemon juice (or juice of ½ lemon)
4 tablespoons soy sauce
1 cup fresh poultry stock, in which 2 tablespoons each of raspberries and blackberries have been cooked for a few minutes and then passed through fine strainer
3-4 fresh basil leaves (cut in large pieces)
salt, freshly ground pepper

Pasta:

6 oz. tomato linguine
6 oz. egg linguine
6-8 quarts boiling, salted, water with
1 tablespoon oil added to prevent pasta from sticking

Garnish:

Spinach leaves, fresh herbs, tomato wedges and edible flowers

To prepare meat croquettes, sauté rabbit on all sides in a hot skillet with a bit of oil; bake in a 400° oven for 6-8 minutes, removing loins before legs and shoulders. Keep medium-rare. When cold, grind rabbit with onion, sorrel, parsley and garlic. In a bowl, add salt and pepper to taste, eggs, flour and pistachios. Shape into balls, about ¾ inch in diameter. Sauté in a little vegetable oil until golden. Bake in a 400° oven for about 5 minutes.

To prepare sauce, place all ingredients in a large skillet. Bring to a boil and simmer for a few minutes.

As you are making the sauce, cook pasta in the boiling water. Pasta should boil 30 seconds to 1 minute depending on the kind of pasta. When cooked as desired (al dente), remove with tongs; toss in the sauce. Add the croquettes and correct seasoning.

Place spinach leaves under pasta as a star. Garnish with fresh herbs, tomato wedges and flowers. Serve immediately.

* skin removed by dipping tomatoes in hot boiling water for a few seconds.

Dominque's Place presents superb French and Northwest cuisine in a charmingly appointed French country setting beside Lake Washington. The recipient of rave reviews and numerous awards, chef Dominique is a master of classic French cooking. This is enriched by his knowledge of international cuisines and his use of only the freshest Northwest produce, poultry, fish, meat and game.

CREDIT CARDS: V, MC, AE, CB, DC, DISC.; WHEELCHAIR ACCESS; BEER/WINE; RESERVATIONS ADVISED

1927 Forty-third Avenue East • (206) 329-6620

THE GREEN LAKE GRILL   SEATTLE

ROAST RABBIT WITH GARLIC AND ROASTED PEPPERS

4 saddles of rabbit, bone removed
2 red peppers, roasted, seeded, and peeled
1 head of garlic, peeled, the cloves left whole
1 cup dry vermouth
1½ cups rabbit or veal stock
¼ lb. unsalted butter, cut into pieces
salt and pepper to taste
2 tablespoons olive oil

Season rabbit with salt and pepper to taste. In a large sauté pan brown the rabbit in the olive oil on both sides. Place in a small roasting pan and place in a 350° oven.

Place the garlic cloves in the sauté pan and quickly brown. Deglaze the pan with the vermouth and bring to a boil. Add the stock and return to a boil. Reduce the liquid to ⅓ cup. While the sauce is reducing cut the peppers into ½-inch strips and add them to the sauce. Whip the butter into the sauce one piece at a time. Serve the sauce over the rabbit.

Serves 4.

The Green Lake Grill is truly one of Seattle's favorites. Owner-chef Karl Beckley offers two distinct rooms and menus, providing both a neighborhood cafe and a formal dining room. During the summer one might have lunch on the lovely patio which provides a great view of Green Lake and the joggers and bikers.

CREDIT CARDS: V, MC, AE; WHEELCHAIR ACCESS; FULL BAR
7850 Greenlake Drive North • (206) 522-3490

CHEZ SHEA

SEATTLE

TENDERLOIN OF BEEF WITH GORGONZOLA SAUCE

Gorgonzola Sauce:

3 tablespoons unsalted butter
5 shallots, minced
3 cloves of garlic, minced
1 cup of Cabernet, Merlot or Zinfandel
1 cup beef stock
2 cups crème fraîche
8 oz. Gorgonzola cheese, crumbled
freshly ground black pepper

Sauté shallots and garlic in butter until translucent. Add wine and stock; cook until reduced by half. Add crème fraîche and reduce again by half. Lower heat and add Gorgonzola, whisking until the cheese is melted and the sauce is very smooth. Transfer to a food processor or blender and pulse. Return to medium heat and simmer gently until desired thickness. Add pepper. Keep warm or reheat when ready to serve.

Carmelized Onions:

4 tablespoons unsalted butter
2 large Walla Walla sweet onions, thinly sliced
4 tablespoons brown sugar

Melt butter in saucepan over medium heat. Reduce heat. Add onions and brown sugar and sauté for about 25 minutes until onions become golden brown and carmelized; set aside.

Tenderloin of Beef:

2 tablespoons of peanut oil
six 6-8 oz. beef tenderloin steaks, each sliced thickly and wrapped with a slice of bacon
¼ cup brandy

Heat oil in large cast iron skillet over high heat. Add steaks. Sauté 3-6 minutes on each side according to desired degree of doneness.

To serve, remove from pan and drain off fat. Deglaze pan with brandy and add carmelized onions. Top each filet with onions and then nap with sauce. Serve immediately.

Serves 6.

With a dozen tables and high-arched windows overlooking Elliot Bay, there is no more intimate or romantic a place in the city. Chez Shea takes full advantage of its location in the Pike Place Market by featuring the wondrous bounty of the Pacific Northwest, and offers a cuisine that rivals the setting.

CREDIT CARDS: V, MC, AE; SMOKING/NON-SMOKING SECTIONS
94 Pike Street, Suite 34, Pike Place Farmer's Market • (206) 467-9990

RAIN CITY GRILL SEATTLE

MIXED SEAFOOD GRILL

1 lb. 8 oz. fresh boned, skinned salmon
1 lb. fresh halibut boned
8 oz. medium prawns (21/30)
8 oz. sea scallops
1½ cups cream
2 eggs
4 tablespoons minced shallots
4 tablespoons minced fresh herbs (basil, thyme, rosemary, fruit sage)
salt and pepper

5-6 feet medium hog casing
8 oz. fresh tuna cut into four 2 oz. pieces
8 oz. fresh salmon cut into four 2 oz. pieces
8 medium prawns
8 large scallops
½ cup rich fish stock
4 red peppers (roasted and peeled)
2 tablespoons minced fresh herbs (primarily basil)
1 pint cream (reduced by ½)

To make sausage, large dice 3-4 oz. of each of the first seafood ingredients and reserve. Push the rest of the first four ingredients through a meat grinder on fine grind. Next, in a food processor, place the ground meat and incorporate the eggs and cream. Then, in a large cold bowl, fold the large-diced seafood, shallots, herbs, and salt and pepper into the ground mixture. This forcemeat may now be stuffed into the casings either by hand or by using the appropriate attachments for the meat grinder. While stuffing, twist casing every 4 inches to make about 4-ounce sausages. Refrigerate until serving time.

For the two sauces, first purée the red peppers and add to a saucepan with the rich stock. Simmer until slightly thickened. For the second sauce, simply add the herbs to the reduced cream and heat slightly.

Meanwhile, poach sauces in a light court boullion. Drain. Grill all of the remaining seafood and poached sausages on a well-oiled grill. Cover ½ of each plate with some of each sauce and arrange grilled seafood and sausage on top. (The sausage may be cut and the casing removed, if desired.)

* The sausage recipe is larger than 4 servings so that it is easier to handle and worth the trouble of making. Uncooked sausage can be kept in the refrigerator 4-5 days or wrapped well, and stored in the freezer for up to 2 months.

Serves 4.

The Rain City Grill's owner Tom Dillard and chef Diana Nowlis, both graduates of the Culinary Institue of America, feature seafood and fresh local produce on their creative menu. Their fresh pastas, poultry and game, and house-made desserts, along with an excellent international wine list, all contribute to making this one of Seattle's memorable restaurants.

CREDIT CARDS: V, MC; WHEELCHAIR ACCESS; SMOKING SECTION; FULL BAR; RESERVATIONS SUGGESTED

2359 Tenth Avenue East • (206) 325-5003

SEA GARDEN
RESTAURANT

CRAB IN BLACK BEAN SAUCE

1 live Dungeness crab (approx. 2 lbs.)
flour
oil
2-3 teaspoons Chinese salted black beans
1 teaspoon minced garlic
2 scallions, chopped
¾ of a medium green bell pepper, diced
2 tablespoons cooking wine
½ cup chicken broth
1 tablespoon cornstarch dissolved in 1 tablespoon water

Peel off top shell of crab. Remove gills inside, and clean crab thoroughly with running water. Split crab in half. Then cut each half into 4 sections, cutting between legs. Coat each piece with a very thin layer of flour. Deep-fry pieces in hot oil for about 1 minute.

Heat a clean wok over high heat. When hot, pour in 2 tablespoons oil. Add black beans and garlic. Stir-fry for ½ minute. Add scallions and green peppers. Stir-fry for ½ minute longer. Add crab and stir thoroughly. Stir in wine and broth. Cover and cook for 1½ minutes. Stir in cornstarch mixture. Cook until sauce thickens. The Crab in Black Bean Sauce is ready to serve.

3-4 servings.

The Sea Garden Seafood Restaurant features Chinese cuisine and especially fresh seafood. The place has tanks filled with live underwater delights, including crab, lobster and Washington State's famed geoduck clams. The customers can even pick the seafood of their choice right out of the tank. This is a favorite with the International District's Chinatown residents. The Sea Garden provides superb food in a simple, bustling neighborhood restaurant with generous servings at reasonable prices.

CREDIT CARDS: V, MC, AE; WHEELCHAIR ACCESS; FULL BAR; RESERVATIONS OPTIONAL
509 Seventh Avenue South • (206) 623-8721

ROVER'S
SEATTLE

PUGET SOUND MELI-MELO

Vermouth Sauce:

½ cup dry vermouth
3 shallots, finely chopped
4 tablespoons veal demi-glaze*
7 tablespoons unsalted butter
salt

16 Penn Cove mussels
16 Manilla or Littleneck clams
12 oz. silver salmon fillet, in 4 pieces
12 oz. ling cod fillet, in 4 pieces

Sea Urchin Flan:

4 oz. sea urchin roe (requires 1-2 sea urchins)
2 egg whites
1 tablespoon heavy cream
white pepper

½ cup dry bread crumbs
8 oz. ocean salad** (Japanese-style
   seaweed salad)

To prepare the vermouth sauce, place dry vermouth and shallots in a saucepan. Reduce liquid by ¾. Add veal demi-glaze* and reduce by ½. Set aside.

To prepare the flan, place sea urchin roe and egg whites in a blender; blend for 30 seconds. Add cream and white pepper to taste; blend 10 seconds more. Pour the flan mixture into four buttered 3 oz. molds or ramekins. Place molds in a shallow baking dish. Pour hot water into the baking dish, halfway up the sides of the flan molds. Cover dish with foil and cook in a 275° oven for about 30 minutes (until just set). Remove from oven and allow to cool in water bath.

Steam mussels and clams to open. Remove and discard top shells. Arrange bottom shells (with meat intact) on a sheet pan, ready for the broiler. Grill salmon and cod until just done. Keep warm.

While the fish is grilling, reheat the vermouth sauce and finish by whisking in the butter. Add salt to taste. (Caution: remember the seafood ingredients have endogenous salts!) Place a dollop of vermouth sauce followed by a sprinkling of bread crumbs over each mussel and clam. Place under a hot broiler until lightly browned. Remove.

To serve, carefully unmold sea urchin flans onto plates. Arrange ocean salad,** cod, salmon, mussels and clams as shown in picture. Surround with remaining sauce and serve immediately.

* Veal demi-glaze is veal stock reduced down to half.

** Ocean salad is available from Mutual Fish Co., Seattle, (206) 322-4368.

Serves 4.

The Rover's atmosphere is warm, quiet, and sophisticated, with still-life paintings gracing its walls. Elegant floral draperies and pale pink walls enhance the spacious, yet intimate, mood of this comfortable home setting. It is the superb artistry of owner-chef Thierry Rautureaus' Northwest cuisine, however, that has established Rover's as one of Seattle's finest restaurants.

CREDIT CARDS: V, MC, AE, DISC.; SMOKING/NON-SMOKING SECTIONS; BEER/WINE; RESERVATIONS REQUIRED

2808 East Madison Street • (206) 325-7442

KOKEB
ETHIOPIAN RESTAURANT   SEATTLE

DORO WAT (CHICKEN STEW)

1 whole chicken, cut into 8 pieces
2 tablespoons strained fresh lemon juice
2 teaspoons salt
2 cup finely chopped onions
¼ cups niter kibbeh (herb butter)*
1 clove garlic, minced
1 tablespoon chopped, scraped fresh ginger root
¼ teaspoon pulverized fenugreek seeds
¼ teaspoon ground cardamon
⅛ teaspoon ground nutmeg (preferably freshly grated)
2-4 tablespoons berbere (red pepper)*
2 tablespoons paprika
¼ cup red wine
1 cup water
4 hard-cooked eggs
½ teaspoon ground black pepper

Pat the chicken dry and rub the pieces with lemon juice and salt. Put the chicken aside. In a heavy 3- to 4-quart enameled casserole dish, cook the onions over moderate heat for 5 or 6 minutes or until they are soft and dry. Stir the onions constantly.

Stir in the niter kebeh and when it begins to splutter, add the garlic, ginger, fenugreek, cardamon, and nutmeg, stirring well after each addition. Add the berbere and paprika, and stir over low heat for 3 to 5 minutes.

Pour in the water and wine, still stirring, and bring over high heat until the liquid in the pan has reduced to the consistency of heavy cream.

Drop the chicken into the simmering sauce, turning the pieces about until they are coated on all sides. Reduce the heat to the lowest point and simmer for 15 minutes.

With the tines of a fork, pierce ¼-inch deep holes over the entire surface of each egg. Then add the eggs and turn them gently about in the sauce. Cover and cook for 15 minutes more, or until the chicken is tender.

* available at the Kokeb Restaurant

Serves 4.

Kokeb, which means "star," is the first Ethiopian restaurant in the Northwest, and is rated the best by many restaurant critics. Since time immemorial, Ethiopia has been famed for its delicious spicy food and hospitality. At Kokeb, they carry on that tradition. The people at Kokeb are pleased to share with you one of their popular recipes so that you, too, at your convenience, may share in Ethiopian tradition.

CREDIT CARDS: V, MC, AE; WHEELCHAIR ACCESS; SMOKING/NON-SMOKING SECTIONS; FULL BAR; RESERVATIONS REQUESTED OVER 4 PEOPLE

926 Twelfth Avenue • (206) 322-0485

CHILE PEPPER

MOLE POBLANO

Mole Sauce:

10 dried ancho chiles
15 dried pasilla chiles
vegetable oil for deep-frying
1 large onion, peeled and cut into
   quarters
8 cloves garlic, peeled
2 cinnamon sticks
7 cloves
7 bay leaves

2 corn tortillas
4 oz. french bread, 1 inch thick
4 oz. chile seeds, reserved from chiles
6 oz. sesame seeds (about 1⅛ cups)
4 oz. roasted peanuts (about ⅔ cup)
chicken broth (about 10-11 cups)
6 boneless chicken breasts, poached in water
   seasoned with onion, bay leaf and garlic
sesame seeds

To prepare sauce, remove seeds from inside chiles and reserve. Deep-fry chiles, one by one, in hot oil. (Just submerge them about 2 seconds to avoid burning.) Then, one by one, deep-fry onion, garlic, tortillas and bread until browned. Deep-fry cinnamon, clove and bay for a second. Drain fried ingredients well.

In a large pan, toast sesame seeds and peanuts. Remove and toast chile seeds.

In a blender or food processor, grind sesame seeds, peanuts and chile seeds with tortillas and bread. Add onion, garlic and spices. Then blend in enough chicken broth to make a medium-thick sauce (about 3 cups broth).

Heat a small amount of shortening in a large pot. Add blended mixture and cook over low heat for 10 minutes, stirring constantly. Add more chicken broth as needed.

Purée chiles with enough chicken broth to make a thick purée (about 3-4 cups). Add to the contents of the pot. Bring to a boil and cook over low heat for 10-15 minutes, stirring constantly. Add more chicken broth as needed. (Sauce should be a little thicker than tomato sauce.) Keep warm, or cool and refrigerate, if made in advance. (Freeze extra sauce if desired.)

To serve, arrange cooked chicken breasts on serving platter. Top with hot Mole Sauce, which has been thinned with a little poaching liquid. Sprinkle with sesame seeds. Accompany with rice and beans, the traditional Mexican way.

6 servings (3 quarts sauce).

Rodolfo Gonzalez, the owner of the authentic Mexican restaurant the Chile Pepper, tells with pride how they opened on May 10, 1985, Mother's Day in Mexico, and how they feature the treasured recipes of his mother Ms. Catalina Mata DeGonzalez. Today they are committed to continuing this tradition of using only the freshest ingredients and preparing each dish with loving care.

NO CREDIT CARDS, CHECKS OK; WHEELCHAIR ACCESS; NON-SMOKING ONLY; BEER/WINE; NO RESERVATIONS

5000 University Way Northeast • (206) 526-5004

THE RITZ CAFE
SEATTLE

HAZELNUT-COATED STUFFED CHICKEN BREASTS

6 whole boneless chicken breasts (or six large bonelees chicken breast halves)
salt and pepper

Stuffing:

1 lb. fresh spinach, washed and stemmed
2 tablespoons butter
3 oz. Dungeness crab meat
2 oz. bay shrimp
¼ cup ricotta cheese
½ cup grated Parmesan cheese
1 egg, beaten

Coating:

flour
3 eggs, beaten
2 cups roasted and ground hazelnuts (or
  seasoned dry bread crumbs)
1 cup oil

Noilly Prat Sauce:

½ cup white wine
½ teaspoons finely chopped garlic
1 teaspoon finely chopped shallots
4 cups cream

salt and white pepper
2 tablespoons Noilly Prat (very dry
  vermouth)

Remove skin and tenders from each chicken breast, leaving in one piece. Cover with plastic wrap and pound out evenly. Season with salt and pepper.

To prepare stuffing, sauté spinach in butter until tender. Drain well, squeezing out excess moisture. Chop. Combine shrimp, crab, ricotta, Parmesan and egg. Fold in spinach. (If mixture seems too soft, add some bread crumbs.)

Place each chicken breast on a level surface and spoon stuffing onto center of each, dividing evenly. Roll up and secure with toothpick. (If using breast halves, enclose stuffing with pointed end, then continue to roll up.) Roll each breast in flour and dip in beaten eggs. Coat with ground nuts. Heat oil. Lightly brown chicken in hot oil to seal. Place on greased baking sheet. Bake in a 375° oven for 25 minutes.

Meanwhile, prepare sauce. Heat a heavy saucepan on high. When very hot, add white wine. Stir in garlic and shallots, cooking a few seconds to release flavor. Add 4 cups cream. Cook until reduced by half or until sauce coats back of spoon. Season to taste with salt and white pepper. Add 2 tablespoons Noilly Prat. Cook a few minutes longer. Strain.

To serve, spoon sauce onto each plate. Slice chicken breast rolls diagonally and fan out over sauce. Accompany with a vegetable and starch. Serves 6.

At the top of Seattle on Capitol Hill is the Ritz Cafe, a center of culinary excitement. This neighborhood gathering spot is known for its inventive cooking, its stunning fruit and cream soups, its chicken and fish, and its weekend breakfasts. The service is meticulous, attentive, and friendly. The piano bar beckons patrons to return again and again.

CREDIT CARDS: V, MC, AE; WHEELCHAIR ACCESS; SMOKING/NON-SMOKING SECTIONS; FULL BAR; RESERVATIONS APPRECIATED

429 - 15th Street East • (206) 328-0440

SAVORY FAIRE

MONTESANO

GRANDMA LOFGREN'S ORANGE RYE BREAD

2-3 tablespoons (envelopes) dry yeast
2 teaspoons sugar
3 cups warm water
10-11 cups all-purpose flour
1 teaspoon anise seed
1 cup water
2-3 teaspoons finely grated orange peel
2 cups light rye flour
¾ cup brown sugar
3 tablespoons shortening
1 tablespoon salt

Dissolve yeast and sugar in warm water. Stir in enough all-purpose flour to make a sponge of the consistency of mud, about 3-3½ cups. Let stand 20 minutes or until bubbly. Meanwhile, combine anise seed, water and orange peel. Bring to a boil and cool to lukewarm. Mix yeast mixture with anise seed mixture. Stir in rye flour, brown sugar, molasses, shortening and salt. Stir in enough all-purpose flour to make a firm dough, about 6-7 cups. Knead 10 minutes on flour surface, adding more flour as needed to prevent dough from sticking. Let rise in a a large bowl, covered, until doubled, about 1-1½ hours. Punch down and divide into thirds. Shape each portion into a round loaf. Place on a greased cookie sheet or jelly roll pan. Cover and let rise until doubled. Slash tops 3 times with a sharp knife or razor blade. Bake at 350° for 40-50 minutes.

Savory Faire is a small cafe and bakery featuring home-cooked food, all made from scratch on the premise. Candi Bachtell who opened Savory Faire in 1986 traces her love of cooking back to her grandmother's restaurant. Perched on a stool in grandmother's restaurant, watching her every move, Candi, still a child, decided to be the family's third generation of restaurateurs. This recipe was generously shared with her by Violet Lofgren whose husband's grandmother brought it from Sweden.

CREDIT CARDS: V, MC; NON-SMOKING SECTION ONLY
135 South Main Street • (206) 249-3701

EL RANCHITO
ZILLAH
EL RANCHITO FAJITAS

1 lb. meat, poultry or seafood of choice
(suggestions: beef sirloin, chicken
breast, pork roast or fresh shrimp)
1 small to medium onion
1 medium tomato
½ green bell pepper
½ red bell pepper
sliced jalapeños or chopped green
chilies to taste (optional)

1 tablespoon cooking oil
6 6-inch El Ranchito flour tortillas,
warmed
hot sauce
guacamole (recipe below)
sour cream

Slice meat or poultry, onion, tomato, peppers and chilies into ling thin slices, ¼-⅜ inch thick. (Slice meat or poultry against grain; peel shrimp and leave whole.) Combine and stir-fry in lightly oiled skillet or wok for 3-5 minutes (do not overcook). Add salt to taste. Serve in warm tortillas. Top as desired, with hot sauce, guacamole or sour cream.

Serves four to six.

El Ranchito Zesty Guacamole:

1 large ripe avocado, mashed
½ diced tomato
1 tablespoon diced onion
1 tablespoon lemon juice
1 tablespoon sour cream
salt to taste

Combine all ingredients. Mix with fork for a chunky sauce, or put in blender for a smooth one.

El Ranchito is a fiesta of taste, smell, sight and sound to delight all the senses. It's a restaurant, bakery, spice shop, gift shop and a tortilla plant all under one roof. Chef Dalia Cruz creates only authentic Mexican dishes, which are enhanced by the presence of colorful piñatas, a beautiful water fountain, and a flower bedecked patio.

NO CREDIT CARDS; WHEELCHAIR ACCESS; BEER; NO RESERVATIONS

1319 East First Avenue • (509) 829-5880

THE SEASONS   PULLMAN

MEDITERRANEAN CHICKEN

2 medium onions, chopped
2 cups celery, chopped
2 large tart green apples
(Granny Smith), thinly
sliced
1 teaspoon salt
1 tablespoon granulated
garlic
5 tablespoons olive oil

white wine
6 large boneless and
skinless chicken breast
halves (or 6 small whole
ones)
2 tablespoons dried Greek
oregano
1 tablespoon dried sweet
basil

6 ounces feta cheese,
crumbled
1 lime (2-3 tablespoons
juice)
2 tablespoons butter
2 tablespoons all-purpose
flour
¼ cup unsweetened apple
cider

Combine onions, celery and apples and lightly sauté in 1 tablespoon olive oil until onions are almost translucent. Sprinkle with a little wine and spoon into a small, deep baking pan. Add 1 cup stock and set aside.

Cover chicken breasts with a layer of clear food wrap and pound to flatten breasts into large, triangular shapes. (Care must be taken to not pound the breast so thin as to separate it; the breast should be uniformly thick but in one piece.)

Arrange flattened breasts on table top with smooth side down. Sprinkle oregano, basil, salt, and garlic on the rough, inner side of the breast.

Crumble the feta cheese over the herbs and spices. Roll the herbs and cheese into the breast starting at the large end of the triangle, ending with the point. Pin the point to the roll with a toothpick.

Dust the outer surface of the rolls with paprika. Heat 2 tablespoons olive oil until very hot in each of two 10-inch skillets. Add chicken breast rolls to hot oil and sauté until medium brown on all sides.

Arrange browned rolls onto chopped vegetables in baking pan and drizzle lime juice over each. Cover pan with foil and bake in 350° preheated oven for 30 minutes.

Melt butter in small saucepan. Once butter is slightly brown, whisk in flour to make a roux; add remaining stock, apple cider, and all of the juices carefully poured from the pan after 30 minutes of baking.

Note: At the Season's Restaurant this dish is served with brown rice, steamed broccoli, cauliflower, red peppers, and carrots. The rice and vegetables are dusted with grated parmesan cheese. The chicken is carefully moved from the baking pan to the plate taking care to include the deep layer of baked vegetables and apples so that they continue to make a nest for the roll. The sauce made from the pan juices is then ladled over the roll and bed of vegetables. The plate is garnished with slices of fresh seasonal fruit.

Chef Craig Dillard, with his commitment to using the freshest ingredients and preparing everything from scratch, has established The Seasons as one of the finests restaurants in the region. Known for its seafood and chicken as well as its "designer special" entrees, the restaurant offers intimate dining with impeccable service. The Seasons, perched atop a flower-covered cliff overlooking downtown Pullman, is an impressive sight complete with stained glass windows.

CREDIT CARDS: V, MC, AE, CB, DC; WHEELCHAIR ACCESS; SMOKING/NON-SMOKING SECTIONS; BEER/WINE; RESERVATIONS ADVISED

Southeast 215 Paradise • (509) 334-1410

STREAMLINER DINER   BAINBRIDGE ISLAND
GREEK PASTA

1 lb. rotini
3 cloves garlic
1 bunch fresh basil (leaves only)
¾ cup sour cream
1 ¼ cups feta cheese (crumbled)
pinch of pepper
1 bunch green onions, sliced wide on the diagonal

1 tomato, sliced into wedges and each wedge sliced in half on the diagonal (or ½ lb. sundried tomatoes)
1 green pepper, diced in large pieces on the diagonal
1 cup Kalamata olives, pitted
6 mushrooms, thickly sliced
2 tablespoons olive oil

Cook rotini; drain and keep warm.

To prepare sauce, blend garlic, basil, sour cream, feta cheese and pepper in food processor. Set aside.

Quickly sauté vegetables in oil until tender-crisp. Toss with rotini. Stir in sauce and serve.

Wine suggestion: a good Beaujolais.

Streamliner Diner features a creative menu with delicious desserts, salads, and unique entrees, all freshly made of the finest ingredients. The warm, colorful island-style restaurant, owned by Alexandra Rust, Judith Weinstock, Irene Clark and Liz Matteson is a local favorite and a destination point at the end of a ferry ride for non-islanders.

CREDIT CARDS: V, MC; WHEELCHAIR ACCESS; NON-SMOKING ONLY; BEER/WINE; NO RESERVATIONS

397 Winslow Way • (206) 842-8495

CAMPAGNE

SEATTLE

VEAL CHOPS STUFFED WITH SWEETBREADS AND MORELS

½ lb. veal sweetbreads
carrot, celery and onion, coarsely diced
bouquet garni
juice of 1 lemon
2 ½ oz. dried morels, reconstituted in
  cold water
2 shallots, minced
2 tablespoons clarified butter

2 tablespoons Madeira
½ cup crème fraîche
1 small bunch chives, chopped
salt, pepper to taste
4 thick cut, pocketed veal chops
1 tablespoon olive oil

Blanch sweetbreads with diced carrot, celery and onion, the bouquet garni and lemon juice. Simmer for 20 minutes. Drain, cool, peel and coarsely chop sweetbreads.

Sauté morels and shallots in clarified butter until translucent. Deglaze the pan with Madeira. Stir in the crème frâiche, chives to taste, and the sweetbreads. Season with salt and pepper. Cool. Stuff the veal chops with the filling.

Brown veal chops well on both sides in a pan in oil and place in a 400° oven for 15 minutes.

Remove from oven, put on a separate plate and keep warm. Prepare sauce.

Sauce:

2 shallots, minced
2 tablespoons clarified butter
¼ cup Madeira
2 cups veal stock

1 ounce morels, reconstituted in cold water
2 tablespoons cold butter
salt, pepper to taste
chives and crème fraîche for garnish

Sauté shallots in clarified butter and deglaze the pan with Madeira. Add the veal stock and morels. Reduce to a glaze and swirl in cold butter over low heat. Season with salt and pepper. Remove veal chops from the oven, place on a serving platter, and pour sauce over veal chops. Garnish with chives and crème fraîche.

Campagne opened in 1985 in a tiny space on Capitol Hill and immediately received rave reviews for the quality of both its food and service. In 1988 Peter Lewis moved Campagne to its present location off the courtyard of the Inn At The Market. Taking her inspiration from the cuisine of Provence, Chef Susan Vanderbeek offers some of the freshest and finest fish, game and produce of the Pacific Northwest. Intimate, sophisticated and yet unpretentious, Campagne features the flavors of Southern France in the heart of Seattle's Pike Place Market.

CREDIT CARDS: V, MC, AE, DC; WHEELCHAIR ACCESS; SMOKING/NON-SMOKING SECTIONS; FULL BAR; RESERVATIONS REQUIRED

86 Pine Street • (206) 728-2800

SOUND FOOD
RESTAURANT AND BAKERY   VASHON

SOUND FOOD CLAM CHOWDER

1 ½ quart clam nectar
2 cups water
2 cups onion, chopped
1 cup celery, chopped
1 cup carrots, chopped
2 medium potatoes, cooked, peeled and diced

Bring nectar, water, and vegetables to boil, covered. Reduce heat, and simmer 10-15 minutes until tender.
Precook potatoes, and prep.

½ pound butter
1 ¼ cup flour

Melt butter until foaming, and whisk in flour until smooth. Cook over medium heat 3-4 minutes. Reserve. This is the roux.

4 cups half and half
12 ounces canned chopped ocean clams of the freshest, best quality possible
¼ teaspoon white pepper
parsley, minced

Add roux all at once to boiling soup when vegetables are tender. Whisk until thick and perfectly smooth. Remove from heat when a boil reaches the surface.
Whisk in half and half and clams. Add white pepper and reserved potatoes and stir well. Garnish with parsley to serve.

8 servings.

Located just seven miles from the ferry landing, Sound Food was established by David and Dorothy Johnson in 1974 to provide the Vashon community with fresh, wholesome food and an informal gathering place. Using the freshest ingredients, Sound Food has developed a reputation for its all-night soup stocks, sauces from scratch, hand-loaved bread from brick-hearth ovens, and its delicate desserts and pastries. There is a constantly changing choice of international, traditional and regional cuisines exquisitely prepared by chef David Hakala. Sound Food's prize-winning garden, wisteria-draped windows and artwork all enhance the fine food it serves.

CREDIT CARDS: V, MC, AE; WHEELCHAIR ACCESS; SMOKING/NON-SMOKING SECTIONS; BEER/WINE; RESERVATIONS RECOMMENDED ON WEEKENDS
20246 Ninety-ninth Avenue Southwest • (206) 463-3565

ALICE'S   TENINO
ALICE'S RESTAURANT BREAD

In a bowl dissolve:

2 tablespoons active dry yeast
2 cups 112° water

Add:

1 tablespoon salt
¼ cup sugar
2 cups white flour

Melt:

¼ cup margarine

Cool slightly and add to the mixture. Mix in:

2 cups whole wheat flour

    Knead in additional flour, alternating ½ cup of whole wheat flour with ½ cup of white flour (a total of about 1½ cups flour each). Knead until dough becomes elastic. Let rise in covered bowl about one hour or until doubled. Pan dough into individual bread pans (about 2½ x 5 inches) with enough dough to almost fill. Let rise until doubled in size. Bake in a convection oven at 400° for 10 minutes or in a regular oven for 10-15 minutes or until browned.

    Yields 15 individual loaves.

Nestled in the Skookumchuck Valley south of Olympia, Alice's Restaurant offers its guests a unique country-style dining experience in a converted rustic red farmhouse Six-course dinners are served in the charming farmhouse—after a visit to taste the excellent hand-crafted wines by Vince deBellis, owner of Johnson Creek Winery. Ann deBellis, a warm hostess, explains the evening's dinner: possibly a magical cream of peanut soup, a plate of rainbow trout, followed by venison, quail, pheasant or rabbit. Delectably rich desserts provide the perfect finale to a delightful country dinner and evening.

CREDIT CARDS: V, MC; WHEELCHAIR ACCESS; SMOKING/NON-SMOKING ROOMS; BEER/WINE; RESERVATIONS REQUIRED

19248 Johnson Creek Road Southeast • (206) 264-2100

CHRISTINA'S   EASTSOUND

SALMON HALIBUT CEVICHE

1 pound freshest salmon, boned and cut into 1 inch cubes
1 pound freshest halibut, boned and cut into 1 inch cubes
½ cup fresh lime juice
1 cup rice wine vinegar
1 - 4 cloves fresh garlic, finely minced
1 tablespoon chopped fresh ginger
½ cup chopped red onion
½ cup chopped red, yellow and green sweet pepper
crushed red chili peppers (optional)
fresh chopped cilantro

   Combine all ingredients in glass, ceramic or plastic container. (Aluminum or any metal must not be used, as it will distort flavor and color.) Chill and marinate, tossing occasionally, for at least four hours or overnight. Serve cold and garnish with chopped fresh cilantro.

On Orcas Island, in the far northwest corner of Washington State, Christina's opened its doors in 1980. Christina Reid-Orchid, owner-chef and Washington native, has received local, statewide and national recognition as an innovative and accomplished chef. Christina's was just chosen one of the region's top three restaurants by readers of Pacific Northwest Magazine. *The restaurant features fresh, local produce in a casually elegant waterfront setting.*

CREDIT CARDS: V, MC, AE, CB, DC; NON-SMOKING SECTION; FULL BAR;
RESERVATIONS SUGGESTED
Porter Building Eastsound • (206) 376-4904

44

CAFE ALEXIS

CAFE ALEXIS SEAFOOD STEW

1 cup dry white wine
1 teaspoon minced garlic
1 tablespoon minced shallots
1 large pinch saffron
1 teaspoon Thai red curry paste
1 teaspoon salt
4 cups fish stock
1 cup coconut milk
1 cup heavy cream
18 Manilla clams — washed

18 mussels — beards removed and washed
18 medium prawns — shelled and deveined
½ lb. firm white fish fillet such as halibut,
   monkfish, or sea bass, cut in 1 inch cubes
½ lb. salmon fillet, cut in 1 inch cubes
1 lb. calamari, cleaned and tubes cut
   in ½" rings
2 tomatoes, peeled, seeded, and diced
¼ cup fine chiffonade of basil leaves

Combine wine, garlic, shallots, saffron, curry paste and salt in a large pan and bring to a boil. Simmer 5 minutes, uncovered. Add fish stock, coconut milk, and cream; bring to a boil and simmer another 15 minutes. Add clams; cover and cook until they begin to open. Add mussels, fish and prawns; cover and cook 3 minutes at a low simmer. Add calamari and tomatoes, bring back to a simmer and cook 1 minute. Stir in basil chiffonade and serve.

Serves six as a main course.

Cafe Alexis is the flagship restaurant of the Hotel Alexis. Chefs Jerry Traunfeld and Emily Moore offer a fresh seasonal menu blending international flavors with their own creations. Because this highly acclaimed cafe seats just 28, every dish at breakfast, lunch and dinner is prepared individually. All meals are graciously served in a charming room with a fireplace and a balcony overlooking Post Alley.

CREDIT CARDS: V, MC, AE, CB, DC; WHEELCHAIR ACCESS; STRICTLY NON-SMOKING; FULL BAR; RESERVATIONS RECOMMENDED

The Alexis Hotel • 1007 First Avenue at Madison • (206) 624-3636

SALVATORE:
RISTORANTE ITALIANO   SEATTLE

POLLO BOSCAIOLA

2 6 oz. boneless chicken breasts
salt
pepper
4 canned artichoke hearts, quartered
8 medium mushrooms, sliced thick
1 clove garlic, finely minced
6 ounces (¾ cup) white wine
4 ounces (½ cup) cream
8 ounces tomato sauce
4 ounces cooked pasta of choice

Lightly flour chicken and season to taste with salt and pepper. Sauté chicken in a little margarine or butter until browned on one side; turn and add vegetables. When vegetables are half-cooked, stir in garlic. When vegetables are golden, add wine. Shake pan; stir in cream and tomato sauce. Cook until sauce thickens. Serve with pasta.

Makes two servings.

In March of 1988 Salvatore Anania opened his highly acclaimed storefront restaurant, bringing to Seattle the 13 years of accumulated knowledge and expertise he had gathered in Italian restaurants in Europe and the United States. Says a connoisseur, "not since Catherine de Medici married Henry II and took her knowledge of great cooking to France has there been such a happy migration of cuisine from one country to another." Heir by background to the richly inventive cooking of Italy's southern regions, Salvatore is a master of other regions as well. In a short time this restaurant has won well-deserved praise from critics and a large loyal following of patrons who rave about his authentic Italian food and wine and his warm, attentive service.

CREDIT CARDS: V, MC; WHEELCHAIR ACCESS; BEER/WINE; NO RESERVATIONS

6100 Roosevelt Way Northeast • (206) 527-9301

CASA MIA
ITALIAN RESTAURANT   OLYMPIA, HOQUIAM

VEAL SCALLOPINE AL MARSALA

6 oz. veal*
2 tablespoons oil
flour
¼ cup light beef stock (we use beef stock rather than veal because of the darker color)
¼ lemon wedge
3 tablespoons sweet Marsala
3 oz. mushrooms (about 1 ½ cups sliced)**

Preheat sauté pan at highest heat with oil until just beginning to smoke, but not burn. Dredge veal scallops liberally in flour and carefully place in sauté pan. The veal will cook very quickly, shrinking as it cooks. Turn when browned, cooking other side. The flour on the veal and the oil in the pan must be balanced so that the veal is not cooking dry, but also so there isn't a pool of oil. Adding more oil may be necessary.

Add stock, tossing to mix; cook until thickened. Squeeze lemon wedge into pan and drop in wedge. Carefully add wine, tossing to mix. Cook until the consistency of medium sauce. Add mushrooms, tossing to mix. Adjust seasonings and sauce consistency.

* We use veal loin (the New York steak piece in beef) cut across the grain, about ⅜ -inch thick. The veal must be very light pink and all connective tissue, fat, etc. trimmed. After slicing, the veal is pounded to about ⅛ -inch thick. You should then have about six veal scallops, around 4 inches in diameter.

** Prior to cooking, select, wash, and dry large white mushrooms. Slice into ⅛ -inch thick slices and set aside.

1 serving.

Casa Mia opened in Hoquiam in 1952. There are now three restaurants. The two newer ones are in Olympia. All are New York style Italian restaurants—typical of those still found in Mulberry St. in Little Italy —and direct descendants of the first pizzeria in this country. Everything is handmade in-house and delicious. The decor and atmosphere is casual and prices are very modest.

CREDIT CARDS: V, MC; WHEELCHAIR ACCESS; SMOKING/NON-SMOKING SECTIONS; BEER/WINE; NO RESERVATIONS

3936 Simspon Avenue • Hoquiam • (206) 352-0440
716 S Plum St • (206) 459-0440 • Olympia • 4426 Martin Wy • (206) 459-0440

SABRINA'S BISTRO — REDMOND
ROULADEN (GERMAN ROLLED AND STUFFED BEEF)

4 slices of top round (about ⅜ " thick x 4" wide, total wt. equals 1½-2 lb.)
4 tablespoons Grey Poupon mustard
1 cup chopped onion
1 cup diced raw bacon
1 dill pickle — cut in 4 long slices
3 or 4 tablespoons shortening
salt
pepper
1 cup water

Tenderize meat, if desired. Spread each slice of meat with 1 tablespoon mustard, ¼ cup onion, and ¼ cup bacon. Lay 1 slice of dill across each piece, then roll up and secure with toothpicks.

Brown meat on all sides in shortening, using a pan which will go in the oven. Season with salt and pepper to taste.

Bake in a 350° oven for 45 minutes. Turn over twice during cooking time, and add 1 cup water after 20 minutes.

Remove meat and make gravy, using a cornstarch flour mixture and pan juices.

Serve with potatoes (mashed), dumplings, or noodles. Accompany with sweet & sour red cabbage, or some other vegetable.

Makes four servings.

A traditional European bistro, owned by Randy and Loretta Hucks, Sabrina's specializes in German and other ethnic cuisines. Chefs Erika Cunnington, from Bavaria, and Rick Diccicco also feature home-made soups, salads, sandwiches, desserts and espresso. Sabrina's catering for all occasions is very popular.

CREDIT CARDS: V, MC, AE; WHEELCHAIR ACCESS; SMOKING/NON-SMOKING SECTIONS
16150 Northeast 85th Street • (206) 883-6204

THE SANTE FE CAFE   SEATTLE

GARLIC CUSTARD

1 cup whipping cream
15 large cloves garlic, peeled

Heat the garlic and cream in a small saucepan over low heat until the cloves are tender, approx. 10 minutes. Do not boil. Puree the garlic and cream in a food processor until the cloves are incorporated into the cream. Meanwhile, in a separate bowl, combine:

4 egg yolks   ½ teaspoon salt
½ teaspoon white pepper   1 teaspoon freshly ground nutmeg

Whisk ingredients together. Mix in the garlic and cream while still hot and blend well. Pour the mixture into 4-ounce custard tins with buttered bottoms (will require three). Place the tins in a shallow roasting pan with water to ¼-inch below the rims. Cover with buttered parchment paper, or a cookie sheet that allows for circulation. Bake at 375° for 40 to 45 minutes, or until the custards are set and golden brown. Remove from the water bath and allow to cool in the molds.

Prior to serving, run a sharp knife around the sides of the tins and invert onto a plate. Place the plate in a hot oven for a minute or two to allow the custards to drop from mold.

To Serve: Pour approx. 2 ounces of Red Chile Montrachet Sauce (recipe below) for each custard on an oven proof serving plate. Place the custard in the center of the sauce. Garnish with a wax paper stencil and red chile powder. Return to the oven to warm before serving. Serve with blue corn tortilla chips or fresh, crusty bread.

Red Chile Montrachet Sauce:

2 ounces plain Montrachet cheese, room temperature.
6 ounces red enchilada sauce. Your favorite or canned.

Put the Montrachet cheese and enchilada sauce (warmed) in the bowl of a food processor with metal blade and blend until smooth.

Wine suggestion: ARBOR CREST Sauvignon Blanc

Sante Fe Cafe owners, Greg, Pam and Steve Gibbons, have enthusiastically enjoyed providing Seattle with the foods of New Mexico since 1981 at their very popular original retreat in the Ravenna neighborhood. Their newer Phinney Ridge location features the same traditional fare and innovative dishes in a charming atmosphere of Southwest color and warmth.

CREDIT CARDS: V, MC; WHEELCHAIR ACCESS; NON-SMOKING THROUGHOUT; FULL BAR; RESERVATIONS FOR PARTIES OF 6 OR MORE

5910 Phinney Ave N • (206) 524-7736 • 2255 NE 65th St. • (206) 783-9755

CAFE BISSETT   FRIDAY HARBOR
ALDER-BROILED BREAST OF CHICKEN

1 cup apple cider
2 tart apples, cored and cut into rings
1 cup rich chicken stock
½ cup whipping cream
6 juniper berries, crushed
3 large chicken breasts, split and boned
2 tablespoons clarified butter

In a brazier, start a fire of alder and allow the fire to burn until a bed of red-hot coals has formed. Meanwhile, prepare the apples and the sauce.

In a deep saucepan, bring the apple cider to a boil. Add the apple rings and let them boil for one minute; then remove them and set them aside. Add the stock to the cider and boil the mixture until it is reduced to one cup. Add the cream and the juniper berries. Continue reducing until the liquid has thickened slightly and become translucent. Keep the sauce warm.

Brush the chicken breasts and the surface of the brazier with clarified butter and broil the chicken skin-side down for five minutes. Turn the breasts and broil them for five minutes more. Turn once again and broil until the breasts are nicely browned and cooked through, about five more minutes.

After the breasts have been turned for the second time, brush the apple rings with butter and broil them for about three minutes on each side. To serve, place the chicken on a plate, top with the sauce and garnish with the apple rings.

Kathleen and David Lee Geist offer guests of Cafe Bissett an experience in dining which is as unique and as appealing as the San Juan Islands themselves. Chefs Kate Wisniewski and Greg Atkinson creatively incorporate fresh and locally produced foods with a variety of entrees which may be accompanied by some excellent regional wines.

CREDIT CARDS: V, MC; WHEELCHAIR ACCESS; SMOKING/NON-SMOKING SECTIONS; BEER/WINE; RESERVATIONS APPRECIATED BUT NOT REQUIRED

First and West Streets • (206) 378-3109

TWO COUNTRIES GRILL   SEATTLE
SZECHUAN BUTTER

Simmer the following ingredients together over low heat for 30 seconds:

¼ pound butter
3 tablespoons soy sauce
1 tablespoon water
1½ teaspoons fresh ginger, ground
1½ teaspoons crushed hot red chili peppers
1 teaspoon fresh garlic, ground
½ teaspoon sesame oil (optional)

Serve 1 ounce (2 tablespoons) over cooked steak, chicken breast, or fish fillets, preferably marinated lightly in equal parts soy, sherry, and corn or peanut oil before cooking. Szechuan Butter holds well in the refrigerator.

The Two Countries Grill offers exotic, unique dishes based on the cuisines of Mexico and China. In their charming 1903 Madrona home, decorated with antiques, owners David Williams and John Sigmon present food that is delicious, artistic, healthy and moderately priced.

CREDIT CARDS: V, MC; SMOKING/NON-SMOKING SECTIONS; BEER/WINE; RESERVATIONS
1416 Thirty-fourth Avenue • (206) 328-2436

THE SHOALWATER RESTAURANT SEAVIEW
GRILLED COLUMBIA RIVER STURGEON

Sturgeon, while one of the ugliest fish you'll ever see, is also one of the tastiest. Similar to chicken in texture and taste, it adapts well to fruity or slightly sweet sauces and grills beautifully.

1 leek, sliced (white part only)
½ green apple, unpeeled and diced
1 red pepper, seeded and diced
2 oz. unpeeled fresh gingerroot, sliced
   into thin 'pennies'
butter
1 cup apple juice or cider

1 cup cream
2 oz. balsamic vinegar
salt and pepper
8 sturgeon fillets (approximately 8 oz. each)
leek 'circles,' sweet pepper strips for garnish

Sauté the leeks, apples, peppers and ginger slices in 2 tablespoons of butter over medium-high heat until the apple begins to fall apart. Add the apple juice and heat the mixture until it begins to simmer. Remove from heat and purée in a blender (be careful not to fill the blender more than halfway — hot liquid explodes out of blenders!). Press as much of the purée as possible through a strainer into a clean saucepan. Add the cream and vinegar to the purée. Add salt and pepper to taste.

Heat the sauce slowly and hold over low heat, until ready to grill the sturgeon. To be safe, place sauce in a bowl over hot water and keep it warm. Brush the sturgeon fillets with melted butter and place on grill; cook until just done. (We like to serve our sturgeon with a touch of pinkness. Be careful not to overcook this fish. It is wonderful and juicy when properly cooked.)

Place a puddle of the warm sauce in the center of the plate. Place the filet on top. Garnish with leek 'circles' and strips of sweet pepper.

The Shoalwater Restaurant at the Shelbourne Inn is located in an historic country inn established in 1896 on the southwest coast of Washington. It offers distinctive Pacific Northwest regional and seasonal cookery exquisitely created by chefs Cheri Walker and Francis Schafer. They work their magic on the region's bounty: seafood, wild mushrooms and berries, game, home-grown herbs and vegetables, all accompanied by selections from an award winning list of 350 wines. From the dining room, with its culinary delights and magnificent wall of leaded and stained glass, to the inn's 16 exquisitely appointed guest rooms, Tony and Ann Kischner's warm hospitality and impeccable service make every visit a truly enchanting experience.

CREDIT CARDS: V, MC, AE; WHEELCHAIR ACCESS; SMOKING/NON-SMOKING; FULL BAR; RESERVATIONS ADVISED

Pacific Highway 103 & North 45 Street • (206) 642-4142

CAFE FELIPE

PAELLA A LA VALENCIA

Spain's most noted dish — it requires a couple of hours of preparation but is well worth it.

6 tablespoons Spanish olive oil
4 cloves garlic, minced
1 lb. Spanish Chorizo (not Mexican) or similar firm sausage, sliced
4 cups short grain white rice
3 tomatoes, cubed
2 white onions, coarsely chopped
¼ cup Spanish dry white wine
1 lemon
8 cups seafood stock (fresh is preferred, but can substitute clam juice if you must)
1 tablespoon salt or to taste

1 teaspoon white pepper
1 teaspoon Spanish saffron
1 teaspoon Spanish paprika
½ cup fresh or frozen peas
¼ cup whole black olives
½ cup Spanish pimientos, sliced thin
10 fresh clams
10 fresh mussels
4 oz. fresh calamari, cut into rings
4 oz. scallops (fresh or frozen)
6 large shrimp
6 chicken thighs, browned beforehand

Paella pan is required for cooking dish — and may be purchased at any kitchen specialty store.

In pan over moderate to high heat, heat olive oil, and brown garlic. Add chorizo and brown a little. Add rice and continue to sauté for 1 minute, coating the rice with the oil. Add tomatoes and onions and wine and continue to sauté until the liquid is reduced somewhat. Add the juice from the lemon; cut half of squeezed lemon in quarters and add to the pan. Add the stock and continue to stir until it reaches the boiling point. Add all your dry spices including the saffron and stir again.

Add the peas, olives, pimientos, and turn the heat down to medium low and let the liquid reduce by at least 20%.

On the surface of the pan alternate clams and mussels (debearded and cleaved) halfway into the rice (bottoms down) around the circumference of the pan. Tuck calamari and scallops into the rice, and arrange the shrimp and chicken over the surface. Bake paella in the oven approximately 25 minutes at 350°.

Garnish with fresh parsley sprigs, and lemon wedges. Olé!

Suggested wine: Monticello Cumbrero 1984

Cafe Felipe, Seattle's leading Spanish restaurant, has gained recognition and popularity over the years for serving what Spain is famous for: paella, tapas and sherry. Owner Maria Monino orchestrates the food, the flamenco, and the setting with such passion that for a few hours you will feel like you've been transported from Seattle's historic Pioneer Square to a remote tablao in Spain.

CREDIT CARDS: V, MC, AE, CB, DC, DISC.; WHEELCHAIR ACCESS; SMOKING/NON-SMOKING SECTIONS; BEER/WINE; RESERVATIONS REQUIRED

303 Occidental Avenue South • (206) 622-1619

THE EMERALD
OF SIAM RESTAURANT   RICHLAND

BLACK RICE PUDDING

½ lb. raw black rice
⅔ cup plus 4 tablespoons sugar
2 tablespoons cornstarch
1 can (14 oz.) coconut cream or cream of coconut
½ teaspoon salt

Wash black rice by rinsing in cold water several times until water is clean. Soak in water overnight. Drain rice; put in a 2 quart saucepan. Add 3 cups water. Bring to boil over high heat. Lower heat but keep water boiling. Cook, uncovered, until rice is tender (about 30-40 minutes).* Add ⅔ cup sugar to rice (reserving 4 tablespoons sugar for sauce). Stir until sugar is dissolved. Stir in cornstarch dissolved in a little cold water. Cook until thickened. Keep warm.

In a small saucepan, heat coconut cream until boiling. Add 4 tablespoons sugar and salt, and continue boiling for one minute. Remove from heat. Serve over the rice in individual bowls.

* Some rice is harder than others and may take a little longer to cook; add more water as needed.

Emerald of Siam provides more than a superb taste of Thai cuisine. Ravadi and Sunanta Lekprichakul are transforming the spacious new facility into an exciting Asian cultural center where cooking, crafts, costumes, music, dance and travel will unite many nationalities within the local community. The Emerald of Siam II was opened in December, 1987, in Kennewick, Washington, at 8300 Gage Boulevard.

CREDIT CARDS: V, MC; WHEELCHAIR ACCESS; SMOKING/NON-SMOKING SECTIONS; BEER/WINE; NO RESERVATIONS

1314 Jadwin Avenue • (509) 946-9328

CREPE DE PARIS

SEATTLE

COUSCOUS

2 tablespoons olive oil
2 racks of lamb
¼ teaspoon ground cumin
¼ teaspoon ground coriander
1 teaspoon black pepper
salt to taste
1 cup couscous
1½ cups boiling chicken stock (seasoned with garlic, parsley, etc.)*
2 tablesoons butter
assortments of seasonal vegetables (asparagus, broccoli, turnip, carrot, etc.)

Heat a heavy sauté pan or cast iron skillet, large enough to hold both racks. Add olive oil. Season lamb with cumin, coriander, pepper and salt; then brown in oil. Place rack in preheated 400° oven, fat side down. Bake 7 - 20 minutes, depending on size.

While lamb is baking, spread couscous in a shallow pan and pour boiling stock over top. Cover pan and let stand 3 - 5 minutes. Mix in butter, with a fork, until all grains are separated.

Steam or cook vegetables as desired. Remove lamb from oven. Allow to rest 4 - 5 minutes. During this time, spread couscous on bottom of each plate. Arrange vegetables around edge. Cut rack of lamb into chops and place in middle of the plate.

*Or use the amount recommended on box of couscous.

Crepe de Paris is best known for the fresh Northwest seafood and poultry done delectably in the Parisian style with touches of nouvelle cuisine by owner-chef Annie Agostini, who comes from Marseille. True to its name, the restaurant serves wonderful and imaginative crepe desserts. The cuisine is complemented by the stunning modern decor, and there is the patio for dining on warm days.

CREDIT CARD: V,MC, AE, CB, DC, DISC; WHEELCHAIR ACCESS; SMOKING/NON-SMOKING; FULL BAR; RESERVATIONS SUGGESTED

1333 Fifth Avenue • Rainier Square • (206) 623-4111

B & O ESPRESSO

SEATTLE

ILONA TORTE

8 egg yolks
3 oz. unsalted butter
1 cup sugar
¼ cup water
5 oz. semi-sweet chocolate
2 cups finely ground walnuts

2 tablespoons fine bread crumbs
8 egg whites
pinch of salt
Ilona frosting (see below)
chopped walnuts

(Have all ingredients at room temperature.)

In mixing bowl, beat egg yolks on high speed until thick and fluffy. Add unsalted butter and continue beating on high until butter and yolks are combined. Beat in walnuts and bread crumbs.

In small pot, bring to boil sugar and water. Remove from heat immediately after boil begins. Add finely chopped semi-sweet chocolate. Stir with spatula until chocolate is completely melted.

Put contents of pan into mixing bowl with beaten yolks and butter. Mix on medium speed, scraping sides of bowl occasionally, until combined.

In separate mixing bowl, beat egg whites and salt until stiff but not dry. Place ⅓ of beaten egg whites into chocolate batter and stir with a spatula to lighten batter. Add remaining whites and fold gently.

Grease and flour 2 9" round cake pans. Pour in batter, dividing evenly. Bake at 350° for approximately 20-25 minutes or until toothpick is no longer wet when inserted into center of cake.

Cool in pans. Then remove carefully. Fill and frost cake with Ilona frosting. Put chopped walnuts around sides.

Ilona Frosting:

4 oz. semi-sweet chocolate
2 tablespoons instant espresso powder
4 teaspoons espresso coffee

½ lb. unsalted butter
⅓ cup powdered sugar
2 egg yolks

Put chocolate, coffee powder and coffee in small pan or in top of double boiler. Melt over hot water, stirring occasionally.

Beat butter, sugar and yolks until light and fluffy. Add chocolate mixture. Beat on high, scraping sides of bowl often, until frosting is light and fluffy. Serves 12.

B & O Espresso has developed a well-earned reputation for its divine desserts, smooth espressos, and gorgeous wedding cakes. Add to this live music, fresh flowers and a unique staff and one knows why B & O Espresso is a favorite Capital Hill institution for cuisine and conversation. They open early and close late, and feature a special weekend breakfast menu. Jane and Majed Lukatah have opened another B & O in West Seattle at 2352 California Avenue S.W.

NO CREDIT CARDS; WHEELCHAIR ACCESS; SMOKING/NON-SMOKING SECTIONS; NO RESERVATIONS

204 Belmont Avenue East • (206) 322-5028

BLACK SWAN RESTAURANT

LA CONNER

PIRATE'S STEW

Sauce:

2 tablespoons extra virgin olive oil
1 each green, red and yellow bell pepper, diced
2 stalks celery, diced
1 Walla Walla sweet onion, diced
2 teaspoons minced garlic
1-3 teaspoons finely chopped hot pepper
2 fresh tomatoes, seeded and diced
1 cup tomato sauce
2 tablespoons capers

1 cup grated Peccorino or Parmesan cheese
1 lb. fresh mixed color pasta sea shells

Seafood:

1 dozen little neck clams
1 dozen Penn Cove mussels, debearded and washed
1 dozen Pin Singing scallops (in the shell)
1 Dungeness crab, sectioned and cracked
1 dozen Hood Canal shrimp, in the shell and trimmed
1 lb. sturgeon fillets, cut into small cubes
1 lb. cleaned squid, body and tentacles
1 small octopus, sliced

To cook pasta, bring a large pot of salted water to boil. Add pasta; cook al dente. Drain and run under cold water. Set aside.

To cook sauce, heat oil in large, heavy bottomed saucepan. Add bell peppers, celery and onion. Sauté but don't brown. Stir in garlic, hot pepper to taste, and tomatoes. Cook 2 minutes. Add tomato sauce and capers. Let simmer while preparing seafood.

To cook seafood, start with the shellfish that takes the longest and continue adding the quicker cooking ones as you go along. Fill a steamer (or a big pot with a lid) with a couple inches of water. Bring water to a boil and add the shellfish: first clams, then mussels, singing scallops, crab and shrimp. As the shellfish nears readiness, add the sturgeon, squid and octopus to the simmering sauce. They will all cook very quickly. Add the shellfish to the sauce as they open. Toss in pasta shells. Arrange on serving plate; sprinkle with grated cheese.

Note: Any Northwest shellfish and seafood can be used, but this is one of our favorite combinations.

In the channelside town of La Conner, the Black Swan Restaurant features the seasonal bounty of local fishermen and the harvest of Skagit Valley. The season might bring fresh local lamb, wild forest mushrooms, woodland greens, or Pirate's Stew, an unabashed celebration of Northwest seafood draped with a fiery Mediterranean sauce.

CREDIT CARDS: V, MC; NON-SMOKING ONLY; BEER/WINE; RESERVATIONS ADVISED
505 South First Street • (206) 466-3040

FLEUR DE LYS

TENDERLOIN MANGO

3 tablespoons cracked black peppercorns
4 8 oz. filet mignons
3 tablespoons butter
6 tablespoons mango chutney
2 oz. (¼ cup) brandy
8 oz. (1 cup) brown sauce (see recipe below)
freshly sliced mango

Press peppercorns onto fillets and lightly salt.

Heat a lightly oiled pan until smoking. Set in fillets. Reduce heat by one-half and cook until almost done as desired.

Add butter and chutney and turn heat back to high. Cook until the butter and chutney bubble and appear shiny. Add brandy. Remove meat and place on serving plate. With sauce still on high heat, add brown sauce and cook until very shiny. Pour over meat. Garnish with mango and serve. Serves 4.

Brown Sauce:

½ lb. veal bones
1 small carrot, finely diced
4 stalks celery, finely diced with no leaves
1 onion rough cut with peelings
½ cup tomato paste
2 cups burgundy
4 tablespoons flour
2 quarts water

1 tablespoon cracked black pepper
1 teaspoon salt
pinch thyme
4 bay leaves
½ bunch parsley
1 teaspoon chopped garlic

Brown bones in a preheated 400° oven on a sheet pan.

In large stock pot cook carrots, celery and onion on medium heat until golden brown. Add tomato paste, burgundy and flour and cook on medium heat for about 5 minutes.

Add water, bones and remaining ingredients; cook for 8 hours on low heat. Add small amounts of water if cooking too rapidly.

Strain sauce through a fine sieve and boil to about 1 quart. (Extra sauce can be frozen.)

The setting of Fleur De Lys is a charming converted 1940's private residence. Jim Jones sole reliance on word-of-mouth advertising has successfully resulted in a long list of patrons who would like the Fleur De Lys to remain a well-kept secret. New guests are warmly welcomed and soon join the patron list. Jim's loyal customers treasure the exquisite dining experience here day or night.

CREDIT CARDS: V, MC; WHEELCHAIR ACCESS; BEER/WINE; RESERVATIONS ADVISED
901 East Legion Way • (206) 754-6208

GASPERETTI'S RESTAURANT   YAKIMA

BRAD'S SUMMER PUDDING

1 pint blackberries
1 pint raspberries
1 pint boysenberries
1 pint red or black currants (see note)
½ cup superfine sugar or enough to sweeten fruit
1 1-lb. loaf country white bread
⅓ cup Grand Marnier
Sauce Anglaise (optional)
lightly-whipped farm cream
1 teaspoon grated orange zest

Place berries and sugar in a medium sized bowl and lightly mix. Set aside for 1 hour or until berries have given off about ¾ cup juice.

Remove crusts from bread. Then cut bread into 2-inch fingers. Line bottom and sides of 6-8 custard cups or a 2-quart souffle dish with bread fingers, cutting slices to fit snugly. Reserve some bread for top. Combine berry juice with Grand Marnier in a small bowl. Brush bread lining with berry juice until well covered.

Spoon berries into bread lining and cover with a bread "lid." Brush top with remaining berry juice and cover with saran wrap. Set a plate or tray on top of the puddings or soufflé dish to weigh them down Place a weight on top so plate or tray fits snugly. Refrigerate for 24 hours.

When ready to serve, remove plate and invert soufflé dish or individual cups onto a serving plate or plates. Nap pudding with Sauce Anglaise, if desired, and serve with the cream into which the grated orange zest has been folded.

Note: Any combination of berries such as loganberries, tay berries, gooseberries, and huckleberries will work in this recipe. Strawberries are not preferred.

6 or more servings.

Gasperetti's has been recognized for over twenty years as one of the most innovative and venerable restaurants in the state. Dining at John Gasperetti's comfortable, intimate establishment is like an old club where you'll be welcomed like a member from your first visit. The daily fresh sheet displays the remarkable skills of chef Brad Patterson whose creativity and consistency continue to amaze customers after two decades of service.

CREDIT CARDS: V, MC, AE; WHEELCHAIR ACCESS; FULL BAR; RESERVATIONS REQUIRED FOR PARTIES OF 5 OR MORE
1013 North First Street • (509) 248-0628

JIMMY B'S CARIBBEAN CAFE

SEATTLE

ISLAND-STYLE COCONUT PRAWNS

3 tablespoons butter
24 large Tiger prawns (about 1 lb.), peeled and deveined
1 red bell pepper, diced in ½-inch pieces
1 yellow bell pepper, diced in ½-inch pieces
1 bunch fresh asparagus spears, blanched and halved
1 tablespoon flour
½ cup white wine
14 oz. canned coconut milk (unsweetened)
1 egg yolk
salt, pepper to taste

Melt butter in sauté pan. Add prawns and bell peppers; sauté until prawns are pink on both sides. Add asparagus and flour; continue sautéing 1 minute longer. Sir in wine to deglaze. Add coconut milk; cook until thick. Remove from heat. Stir in egg yolk. Season with salt and pepper.

Jimmy B's Caribbean Cafe features the finest in Caribbean food, atmosphere and tropical libations right on Seattle's waterfront. Jimmy B's has great outdoor dining, weather permitting, and dancing to live music, island style, on weekends. Owner Mark Hesch says, "Come, relax at our Island in the City."

V, MC, AE, CB, DC; WHEELCHAIR ACCESS; SMOKING/NON-SMOKING; FULL BAR; RESERVATIONS RECOMMEND

2815 Alaskan Way • Pier 70 • (206) 728-9221

THE GEORGIAN ROOM SEATTLE
BEEF MEDALLIONS WITH SHALLOT AND MUSTARD CRUST

16 oz. beef tenderloin, cut into 8 - 2 oz. pieces
6 teaspoons chopped shallots
4 teaspoons chopped parsley
3 teaspoons Dijon mustard
1 egg yolk
1 teaspoon all purpose flour
1 English cucumber, peeled, seeded and cut into ¼" x 1" strips
2 candy beets, peeled and sliced very thin *
salt and pepper to taste
3 tablespoons olive oil
3 large pieces Belgian endive
3 tablespoons veal or chicken broth
½ cup heavy cream
dash of nutmeg

Combine shallots, parsley, mustard and egg yolk. Slowly add flour and blend. In small skillet, cook bacon until golden. Pour off three-quarters of fat. Add cucumber and beets and sauté on medium high heat approximately 1-2 minutes or until tender. Set aside.

Sprinkle meat with salt and pepper. Place 1 tablespoon of mustard mixture on each 2 ounces piece of tenderloin. Heat large skillet with the olive oil until hot. Place each piece of meat in skillet, mustard side down. Reduce heat immediately to medium low. Cook all pieces until mustard side is golden brown. Turn medallions over and turn heat off. After 2-3 minutes, remove medallions from pan and keep warm.

Core endive and separate leaves. Heat skillet on medium high heat. Add a touch of butter. Add endive with 3 tablespoons broth. Cook about 20 seconds. Add cream and nutmeg. Mix together gently.

Place cucumber mixture in center of plate, medallions on top, and surround with endive mixture.

* a variety of beet that is very small and has a variegated color

The Georgian Room in the Four Seasons Olympic Hotel, in all its elegant splendor, with floor to ceiling windows, sparkling beaded crystal chandeliers, lofty ceilings and silver appointments, is a setting fit for dinners of state. Executive Chef Ludger Szmania's mastery of cooking presents a creative, fresh regional menu offering: for example, rack of Ellensburg Lamb with baked goat cheese in filo dough, or smoked planked salmon with apple cider sauce. The Georgian Room prides itself on providing one of Seattle's most elegant downtown luncheons, a famous and lavish Sunday brunch, and those "power breakfasts." The gracious, attentive service enhances a grand dining experience morning, noon and evening.

CREDIT CARDS: V, MC, AE, CB, DC; WHEELCHAIR ACCESS; SMOKING/NON-SMOKING; FULL BAR; RESERVATIONS REQUIRED; COMPLIMENTARY VALET PARKING
Four Seasons Olympic Hotel, 411 University Street • (206) 621-1700

INNISFREE   DEMING

BUTTERNUT/APPLE BISQUE

1 large butternut squash (about 2½ lbs.)
2 tablespoons butter
1 large onion
2 stalks celery
2 medium Washington grown apples (i.e. Melrose, Spartan, Jonagold)
1 quart homemade chicken stock
salt, pepper, parsley, dill, nutmeg
Crème Fraîche
fresh chopped parsley or a sprig of dill

Peel and cut squash into 2-inch cubes, removing pulpy center. Quarter and core apples. Peel and finely chop onions and celery.

Melt butter and sauté onions in large stock pot until onions are barely translucent, stirring occasionally. Add celery and cook three minutes more. Add squash and enough stock to entirely cover vegetables.

Add salt, pepper, parsley, dill and nutmeg to taste. Cover pot and simmer until squash is fork tender, adding apples during last ten minutes of cooking.

Purée soup in batches in a food processor, or in the stockpot with a Bamix or Braun type mixer.

Add more chicken stock if thinner consistency is desired.

Serve in a heated bowl with a dollop of crème fraîche and a sprinkling of parsley or dill.

To make this a "heart-healthy" meal, substitute olive oil for the butter and low fat yogurt for the crème fraîche. When making your own chicken stock, be sure to strain, cool, and skim all fat off top of stock.

Serve with fresh baked bread.

6 servings.

Suggested wine: Mt. Baker Vineyards Madeline Angeuine

Innisfree was established in 1984 in the scenic foothills of Mount Baker as a culinary extension of Fred and Lynn Berman's own 20 acre organic farm. The Bermans are committed to sustainable agriculture and regional self-sufficiency, and patrons find this dramatically expressed in an ever-changing but always extraordinary menu that features seasonal Pacific Northwest ingredients.

CREDIT CARDS: V, MC; WHEELCHAIR ACCESS; NON-SMOKING ONLY; BEER/WINE; RESERVATIONS SUGGESTED

9393 Mt. Baker Highway • (206) 599-2373

GIORGINA'S
SEATTLE

GIORGINA'S PIZZA

Pizza Dough:

2 packets dry yeast
2 cups warm water
5-5½ cups flour
1 teaspoon salt

Pizza Sauce:

1 (28 oz.) can Italian plum tomato purée
1 teaspoon salt
½ teaspoon fresh ground black pepper
2 teaspoons dried oregano
water to thin

Toppings (in order of placement):

½ cup grated Parmesan cheese
1 lb. whole milk mozzarella cheese, coarsely grated
2 cups white onion rings, cut paper thin
⅔ lb. pepperoni (purchase natural casing pepperoni from a good Italian deli and have them slice it thin)
2 green peppers, cut in 1-inch squares (coat with olive oil; bake in a hot oven until soft; drain and cool)

¼ lb. sliced mushrooms (sauté in olive oil for two minutes; season with pepper; cool and drain)
sausage (Mix together 1 lb. fresh, 80% lean ground pork with 2 tablespoons cracked fennel, 1 tablespoon paprika, 1 teaspoon black pepper, 2 teaspoons salt, and ¼-½ teaspoon red pepper flakes. Shape into small balls.)

Dissolve yeast in warm water. With a wooden spoon, stir in ⅔ of flour, and when well mixed, turn onto a floured board. Sprinkle salt onto dough. Knead for 15 minutes, adding just enough flour to prevent sticking. After kneading, the dough will be light in texture and will gently bounce back when touched.

Put a teaspoon of olive oil in a large bowl. Roll dough in oil to coat. Cover with a cloth and place in a warm, draft-free location. Let rise until doubled.

Meanwhile, prepare sauce and toppings. For sauce, whisk together ingredients. Simmer 20 minutes, covered. Cool. Prepare toppings as directed.

Coat 2 large baking tins with olive oil. Preheat oven to 475°. Divide dough in half. Press each ball of dough out flat with hand to a 16-inch round, about ¼ inch thick. Use rolling pin, if necessary. Transfer to the oiled tin. Cover with a cloth and let rise on top of oven for 10 minutes. The dough should be ¼ to ½ inch thick and even throughout.

Spread each pizza with 12 oz. (1½ cups) sauce, using a flat spoon. Go over the edges and onto the pan. (No white from the dough should be visible.) Add toppings in order given, using ½ for each pizza. Bake for 15-20 minutes or until cheese and toppings in center are cooked and browned. 6-8 servings (2 16-inch pizzas).

Giorgina's is neighborhood friendliness plus Capital Hill pizazz with gourmet quality. Marlis Korber's unique and incredibly good pizza is built on original Italian-styled, twice-risen dough with naturally flavored sauces, roasted or sautéed vegetables, top-of-the line fresh pork, great anchovies, and true Canadian bacon, all prepared in the house.

CREDIT CARDS: V, MC; WHEELCHAIR ACCESS; SMOKING/NON-SMOKING SECTIONS; BEER/WINE; NO RESERVATIONS

131 - 15th Avenue East • (206) 329-8118

il fiasco

COZZE ALA ARANCIONE

12 oz. bearded mussels
1 oz. butter
½ teaspoon shallots, chopped
2 tablespoons leeks, sliced
⅛ cup Tuaca
¼ cup fresh squeezed orange juice
½ cup heavy cream
3 tablespoons peeled, seeded, and chopped tomato
salt, white pepper
½ teaspoon chopped parsley
¼ teaspoon orange zest

Sauté shallots and leeks in butter over low heat until lightly wilted, about 2 minutes. Add Tuaca, orange juice and mussels. Cover and steam. Remove mussels when opened and keep warm. Add cream to sauce; reduce over high heat by one-third. Add tomatoes, parsley, salt, and white pepper to taste. Heat through. Pour over mussels. Sprinkle with orange zest and fresh watercress.

Arrange mussels, open shell up. Do not completely cover with sauce.

In Italian "il fiasco" is a large bottle of wine, usually straw-covered. Owned by Teri Treat and chef Dave Nelson, this very elegant yet intimate restaurant is considered one of the best in Bellingham. They also do catering with a completely Italian focus.

CREDIT CARDS: V, MC; WHEELCHAIR ACCESS; FULL BAR; RESERVATIONS SUGGESTED
1309 Commercial Street • (206) 676-9136

GRAND PALACE
SEATTLE

PAD PALI

¼ cup oil
6 fresh clams, cleaned
6 small mussels, cleaned
2 large cloves garlic, chopped
¼ cup red pepper strips
¼ cup green pepper strips
1 small onion, sliced
¼ cup sliced bamboo shoots
¼ cup canned straw mushrooms
6 prawns, shelled and deveined
¼ cup scallops
3 oz. red snapper fillet, sliced
3 tablespoons fish sauce
2 tablespoons sugar
1 tablespoons oyster sauce
½ teaspoon white pepper
cilantro for garnish

Heat skillet over medium heat and add oil. When oil is hot, add clams and mussels. Cook until clams and mussels open. Add garlic and sliced vegetables. Cook for ½ minute. Add remaining ingredients except cilantro. Stir lightly. Then turn heat to high. Continue cooking until all seafood is cooked. Garnish with cilantro or more red and green pepper slices.

4 servings (as part of a Thai meal).

Grand Palace's owner-chef, Rut Poladitmontri, serves tradtional yet highly creative recipes, blending the exotic, fiery tastes of Thailand with the freshest ingredients of the Pacific Northwest. A chef in great demand, Poladitmontri has a loyal following from the Uwajimaya Cooking School, and he has his own product line of sauces and curry pastes. The flavors of Thailand in the masterful hands of Chef Rut are also now available at his new restaurant, The Lemon Grass Grill, 7200 E. Greenlake Drive.

CREDIT CARDS: V, MC; WHEELCHAIR ACCESS; SMOKING/NON-SMOKING SECTIONS; BEER/WINE; RESERVATIONS NOT REQUIRED

417 Second Avenue • (206) 624-3825

CHINA NORTH RESTAURANT SEATTLE

ORANGE-FLAVORED BEEF

½ lb. flank steak, cut in slices approximately 2 inches long, 1 inch wide and
  ⅓ inch thick
cornstarch for coating
oil
2 slices fresh ginger, minced
3 green onions (white part only), cut in ¼-inch pieces
orange rind (from a 4-inch orange), cut in pieces a little smaller than the beef
3 tablespoons soy sauce
1 tablespoon white cooking wine
1 teaspoon vinegar
1½ tablespoon sugar
1½ tablespoon water
½ tablespoon cornstarch dissolved in ½ tablespoon water
fresh orange slices

Dip individual slices of beef in cornstarch to coat lightly. Heat 2 cups oil in wok on high. Deep-fry beef slices until light golden brown. Drain. Remove all but 1 tablespoon oil from wok. Return to high heat. Add ginger, green onions and orange rind. Stir-fry 4-5 times. Add remaining ingredients except cornstarch mixture and orange slices. Bring to a boil. Stir in cornstarch mixture. Add beef, stirring 2-3 times to coat evenly. Spoon into serving dish. Garnish with orange slices.

4 servings (as part of a Chinese meal).

China North prides itself on being the only Chinese restaurant in the Northwest which presents an authentic Imperial Banquet upon request. This is a twelve-course meal prepared just as the Emperor requested centuries ago. They were chosen as the official restaurant for the "Son of Heaven" imperial arts of China exhibit. Tom Chi, the chef, has many years experience in the art of Chinese cooking and he's highly regarded for his hand food carving.

CREDIT CARDS: V, MC; WHEELCHAIR ACCESS; SMOKING/NON-SMOKING SECTIONS; BEER/WINE; RESERVATIONS SUGGESTED

12314 Roosevelt Way Northeast • (206) 362-3422

ITALIA

SEATTLE

PETTI DI POLLO COI CAPRINI

This is a simple dish to prepare and cook. It makes an excellent one-course meal. Great for summer parties.

8 basil leaves, julienned
2 oz. fresh goat cheese (Montrachet or something similar)
1 teaspoon fresh lemon zest
1 whole boneless chicken breast with skin on
salt and pepper
assorted wild greens
vinegar and oil dressing
edible flowers for garnish

In a small bowl mix ¾ of the julienned basil, goat cheese, and lemon zest. Divide chicken breast in half lengthwise. Form a pocket under the skin and above the chicken meat with your finger or a small knife. Stuff equal amounts of the goat cheese-basil mixture in the pockets under the skin of each breast. Salt and pepper the chicken on both sides.

Grill the breasts on a barbecue with medium hot coals for about 4 mintues on each side. If not using a barbecue, you can bake the breasts in a small casserole dish for 15 minutes in a preheated oven at 375°, skin side up.

Toss the wild greens with a vinegar and oil based dressing. (We use Italia's house vinaigrette which includes Dijon mustard.) Distribute the greens on two large plates. Allow the chicken breasts to cool down a bit. The breasts can be served either sliced or whole on the bed of greens. Garnish with remaining basil and edible flowers.

Italia is more than an evening cafe featuring imaginative, regional Italian cuisine that takes full advantage of fresh local products. Italia is also an enoteca (wine bar), a pasta bar, a full-service deli and catering facility, a gourmet grocery, an import gift shop and a contemporary Northwest art gallery. These are all skillfully orchestrated by David Holt and Paul Schell. In addition, Italia plays host to a great variety of special events featuring artist's groups.

CREDIT CARDS: V, MC, AE, CB, DC; WHEELCHAIR ACCESS; SMOKING/NON-SMOKING SECTIONS; BEER/WINE; RESERVATIONS SUGGESTED

1010 Western Avenue • (206) 623-1917

MILFORD'S FISH
HOUSE AND OYSTER BAR
SPOKANE

MILFORD'S GREEK SAUTE

¼ cup butter
6 oz. fresh Ahi (yellowfin tuna), cut into ½-inch chunks (or other varieties such as ono,
  marlin, swordfish, mahi mahi, or halibut)
⅔ cup sliced mushrooms
¼ cup sliced black olives
1 cup diced tomatoes
1 teaspoon minced garlic
1 teaspoon dried basil
2 tablespoons white wine
2 green onions, diced
1 oz. feta cheese, crumbled (about 3 tablespoons)
pinch of chopped parsley
lemon wedge

In a small sauté pan, melt butter. Add tuna and mushrooms and sauté slightly.
Add olives, tomatoes, garlic, basil and wine. Sauté until fish is done. Fold in green
onions and feta cheese. Serve over rice in a round bowl with a rim. Garnish with
parsley and lemon wedge.

This recipe makes 1 portion as served in the restaurant. For more servings, adjust
accordingly.

*Milford's Fish House and Oyster Bar has lived up to its commitment to serve the very
highest quality seafood since it opened in 1980. Brick walls, gleaming hardwood floors,
ceiling fans and red checkered tablecloths set the scene for dinners in a casually elegant
atmosphere reminiscent of the Tadich Grill in San Francisco. Chef Dave Jones is also
one of the owners. Milford's features a wonderful variety of Northwest seafood dishes
which change daily according to seasonal availability and price.*

CREDIT CARDS: V, MC, AE; WHEELCHAIR ACCESS; FULL BAR; RESERVATIONS RECOMMENDED
North 719 Monroe Street • (509) 326-7251

GHENGIS KHAN   SEATTLE
KUNG PAO CHICKEN

8 oz. boneless chicken meat
¾ teaspoon salt
1 teaspoon flour
1½ teaspoons sesame oil
1 tablespoon vegetable oil
3 oz. raw peanuts (about ½ cup)
½ teaspoon diced garlic
15 small, dried, red hot peppers
½ teaspoon soy sauce
½ teaspoon oyster sauce
½ teaspoon red hot pepper sauce
2 teaspoons sugar

Remove the skin and fat from chicken and slice thinly. Toss with ¼ teaspoon of the salt, 1 teaspoon of the sesame oil and 1 tablespoon vegetable oil. Let marinate 1 hour.

Pour 20 oz. of oil into a hot wok. Heat oil to medium, about 150°. Add peanuts; stir slowly until peanuts turn light brown. Use a strainer to remove peanuts from oil.

Leave oil in wok. Turn heat to high. When oil is very hot, add chicken and stir. Be sure chicken is separated and not sticking together. Stir until chicken is almost cooked, about 2 minutes. Remove with a strainer. Empty out oil.

Reheat wok over high heat. Add 1 tablespoon oil. When hot, add garlic. Stir in hot peppers, chicken, peanuts, ½ teaspoon of the salt, soy sauce, oyster sauce and hot pepper sauce. Add sugar; mix well. Then stir in ½ teaspoon sesame oil. Serve on plate.

Serves 4.

Genghis Khan serves only authentic Szechuan and Cantonese cuisine. The head chef from mainland China is very knowledgeable and adept at creating both spicy and non-spicy styles. Mr. Lew is an attentive host in this attractive restaurant located near the Pike Place Market.

CREDIT CARDS: V, MC, AE, DISC; WHEELCHAIR ACCESS; SMOKING/NON-SMOKING SECTIONS; BEER/WINE; RESERVATIONS REQUIRED

1422 First Avenue • (206) 682-3606

AT THE LAKESIDE
SEATTLE

ROQUEFORT NEW YORK

2 tablespoons green peppercorns, rinsed
4 tablespoons oil
4 New York steaks
2 medium garlic cloves, minced
1 cup tawny port
⅔ cup whipping cream
⅔ cup Roquefort cheese, crumbled

Crush peppercorns and set aside. Heat oil in pan over medium-high heat. Sear steaks about 3-4 minutes on a side. Set aside and keep warm.

In same pan, add garlic, peppercorns and port. Bring to a boil over high heat. Add cream and stir constantly until mixture is reduced by half. Stir in Roquefort cheese until cheese melts. Make 4 slashes evenly spaced on each steak, cutting ¾ of the way through. Fill each pocket with Roquefort sauce, spooning remaining sauce over top.

At The Lakeside is another Seattle restaurant created by Dan and Cecily Sandal. It is set on the north end of Lake Union, commanding the finest view of downtown. Their cuisine emphasizes the Northwest's choicest bounty of seafood, plus a tantalizing choice of poultry, beef and lamb dishes.

CREDIT CARDS: V, MC, AE; SMOKING/NON-SMOKING SECTIONS; FULL BAR; RESERVATIONS REQUIRED

2501 North Northlake Way • (206) 634-0823

THE 1904 RESTAURANT/BAR

SEATTLE

WHITE KING SALMON

½ bottle dry champagne (sparkling wine)
2 shallots, finely chopped
4 oz. wild huckleberries (save a few for garnish)
½ lb. cold butter
lemon juice
6 5 oz. pieces fresh White King salmon filet
salt and freshly ground pepper
2 tablespoons clarified butter
lemon slices

Sauce: In a small sauce pan add finely chopped shallots and the huckleberries (saving a few for garnish). Reduce on low heat until only ½ cup of liquid remains.

Strain this reduced liquid into a second sauce pan through cheesecloth by pressing gently with a rubber spatula to force some of the berry pulp through the cloth.

Place this second sauce pan on very low heat and wisk in the cold butter one teaspoon at a time. When half of the butter is incorporated, remove from heat and continue to add the remaining butter. After all the butter has been incorporated, the sauce should be slightly thick; (if not, add a few more teaspoons of cold butter). Add a dash of lemon juice and set aside in a warm place on the stove.

Fish: Preheat oven to 500°. Sauté the salmon which has been seasoned with salt and freshly ground pepper in the clarified butter until the fish is lightly brown on one side. Turn the fish over and bake in the oven at 500° for 3-4 minutes. Do not overcook the fish.

Cover the middle of the plates with the sauce and place the salmon fillets in the middle of the plate on top of the sauce. Garnish with remaining huckleberries and lemon slices.

Serves 6.

One of Seattle's finest downtown restaurants, The 1904 Restaurant/Bar is known for its imaginatively prepared seafood that is inspired by French and Italian cuisine. With a strong emphasis on fresh Northwest bounty, David Holt offers lunch and dinner in a classic urban setting enhanced by award-winning architecture. Happy Hour provides half-priced appetizers, including The 1904's renowned carpaccio.

SMOKING/NON-SMOKING SECTIONS; FULL BAR
1904 Fourth Avenue • (206) 682-4142

MARRAKESH
MOROCCAN RESTAURANT SEATTLE

SALMON "MARRAKESH"

3½-4 pound whole salmon (or cod fillet, seabass or white fish fillets), scaled and
  cleaned
½ cup of olive oil
3 cloves garlic, finely minced
1 teaspoon white pepper
3 teaspoons paprika (Hungarian)
1 teaspoon salt
1 teaspoon ground cumin
½ bunch finely chopped parsley
½ bunch finely chopped cilantro (Chinese parsley)
4 firm ripe tomatoes thinly sliced
2 lbs. potatoes, peeled and thinly sliced (optional)
2 green peppers cored, seeded and cut into juliennes
2 medium onions, peeled and finely minced

Place the salmon in a large non-stick baking pan.

In a small bowl, combine olive oil, garlic, white pepper, paprika, salt, cumin,
parsley and cilantro. Mix well and pour one-half the amount over surface of salmon.
Place sliced tomatoes, potatoes, peppers and onions on fish, arranging them evenly
over the top; then pour the remaining half of seasoning mixture over the vegetables.

Bake at in 400° for 30-45 minutes (25-30 minutes for fillets), or until fish is done.
Salmon may be served directly from the baking pan.

4-6 servings.

*In the traditional code of Moroccan hospitality, all guests at the Marrakesh are treated
with graciousness and attentiveness. At this cozy yet upscale oasis of quiet good taste host
Ben Alaoui, owner and head chef, offers the finest in classic Moroccan cuisine. An
added delight is the traditional belly dancing.*

CREDIT CARDS: V, MC, AE, CB, DC; WHEELCHAIR ACCESS; SMOKING/NON-SMOKING SECTIONS;
FULL BAR; RESERVATIONS REQUIRED

605 - 15th Avenue East • (206) 328-4577

MIRABEAU   SEATTLE
ROAST BONELESS LAMB LOIN WITH ROSEMARY DEMIGLACE

1 whole lamb loin, boned
2 onions, quartered
3 cloves garlic, chopped
1 carrot, chopped
2 celery stalks, chopped
2 bay leaves
6 peppercorns
parsley stems
½ cup good red wine

¼ cup red wine vinegar
1 shallot, chopped
3 tablespoons olive oil
1 cup roasted pinenuts
2 cups dried bread crumbs
1 tablespoon fresh rosemary, chopped
salt and pepper
1 teaspoon Dijon mustard

Ask your butcher to remove the fat and silver skin from the lamb loin. All that should be left are two perfectly clean cylinders of lamb. Also ask for additional lamb bones, or purchase a few lamb shanks to enrich the lamb stock.

In a roasting pan, place the bones from the lamb loin plus any additional bones, onions, garlic cloves, carrot, and celery stalks. Place in a 400° oven until bones and mirepoix are brown. Remove bones and mirepoix to a 3-gallon stockpot, discarding any grease. Add two bay leaves, six peppercorns and some parsley stems and cover bones with 2½ gallons of water. Bring to a boil and simmer for 24 hours, skimming the fat and residue from the top occasionally.

Strain stock through a fine chinois into another pot and reduce until it coats the back of a spoon. Meanwhile, in a small saucepan bring to a simmer red wine, red wine vinegar, shallot, and rosemary. Add the reduced stock and continue to reduce until you have approximately 2 cups of liquid. Strain through a fine chinois and adjust seasonings. Set aside rosemary demiglace while preparing lamb.

In a food processor, place pinenuts and bread crumbs and chop until fine. Rub lamb loins with 1 tablespoon olive oil and season with salt and pepper. Rub top of loin with mustard, then dredge in pinenuts and bread crumbs.

In a large sauté pan, heat 2 tablespoons olive oil. Sear lamb loins, first on one side, then turn (approximately 2 minutes per side). Place pan in a 400° oven for about 10 minutes. Remove to a warm, but not hot, place and allow to stand an additional 5 minutes before slicing. Carve and place on top of rosemary demiglace. Garnish with roasted garlic cloves, finely diced red bell peppers, steamed spinach and fresh rosemary.

Serves 4.

Mirabeau combines four-star dining with a spectacular view of Puget Sound. Tom Cosgrove and Paul Abodeely's comfortable, elegant 46th floor restaurant offers a sweeping view of Mount Rainier, the Olympic Range and the Space Needle. Relax with a cocktail in the attractive lounge, or visit the dining room for chef Jeff McClelland's superb Northwest and continental cuisine.

CREDIT CARDS: V, MC, AE, CB, DC; WHEELCHAIR ACCESS; SMOKING/NON-SMOKING SECTIONS; FULL BAR; RESERVATIONS RECOMMENDED

1001 Fourth Avenue Plaza, 46th Floor • (206) 624-4550.

BIRCHFIELD MANOR   YAKIMA

BIRCHFIELD MANOR CASSATA

⅓ cup water
sugar
2 cups ricotta cheese
3 tablespoons whipping cream
4 tablespoons Grand Marnier
¼ cup finely chopped candied fruit
1 lb. semisweet chocolate, chopped
¾ cup black coffee
1 loaf lemon-flavored poundcake (from your favorite recipe or bakery)
2 cubes (½ lb.) unsalted butter

To prepare syrup, combine water and ⅔ cup sugar. Bring to boil; then cool. Add 2 tablespoons Grand Marnier and set aside.

To prepare filling, place ricotta cheese in food processor. Process until smooth. Add whipping cream, 2 tablespoons Grand Marnier and ¼ cup sugar. Continue processing until smooth. Mix in candied fruit and ¼ lb. of the chopped chocolate.

To assemble cake, cut poundcake into 3 slices lengthwise, to make layers. Place bottom layer on a board or cake plate. Brush with syrup. Spread with half of filling. Top with center layer, more syrup and remaining filling. Cover with top layer. Brush with syrup. Wrap in plastic and refrigerate while preparing icing.

For icing, combine coffee and 12 oz. chopped chocolate. Heat gently until melted. Remove from heat. Cut butter into small pieces and add to coffee mixture. Stir until melted. Let cool until it reaches spreading consistency. Completely cover top and sides of cake with icing. Chill. Cake is best when made a day ahead and refrigerated. Remove from refrigerator 2 hours before serving.

Serves 8 - 10.

Built in 1910, this mansion has been called a Victorian jewel in the Yakima desert. Dining at the Birchfield Manor with Wil and Sandy Masset, who bought the two-and-a-half-story mansion in 1979, is like stepping back in time to have a gracious dinner party with friends. The food is exceptional. Every dish is prepared with the freshest, hand selected ingredients by European-trained chef Wil Masset. Menu selections include classic international cuisine with a variety of original and regional specialties. Wil will personally escort you on a tour of their extensive wine cellar and offer irresistible suggestions. From the crystal chandeliers to the winding staircase leading to antique-filled guest rooms, this jewel from the past is still one of Washington's treasures today.

CREDIT CARDS: V, MC, AE; WINE
2018 Birchfield Road • (509) 452-1960

ARITA RESTAURANT SEATTLE
TERIYAKI SAUCE

1 cup Mirin (Japanese sweet cooking wine)
1 cup soy sauce
1-2 slices fresh ginger
1-2 cloves garlic, minced

Pour Mirin into a small pan. Heat to boiling and continue to cook a few minutes to remove alcohol. Add soy sauce, ginger and garlic. Cook a few minutes longer.

To serve, spoon warm sauce over grilled chicken or fish. Extra sauce may be refrigerated.

Makes about 1½ cups.

Owner-chef Daiki Matsueda's eighteen years of cooking experience in his native Japan and in this country is reflected in the traditional Japanese food prepared from original recipes with his unique techniques. He and his wife opened this delightful restaurant two years ago, and one visit will show why Arita's reputation and popularity have grown so quickly.

V, MC; WHEELCHAIR ACCESS; SMOKING/NONSMOKING SECTIONS; BEER/WINE
8202 Greenwood Avenue North • (206) 784-2625

LONGFELLOW CAFE
MT. VERNON

PASTA PEMAFLORA

8 oz. fresh pasta of choice
⅛ cup olive oil
2 shallots, minced
salt, freshly ground pepper
½ cup chicken stock
4 slices julienned red pepper
¾ cup whipping cream
1 tablespoon flowers and/or herbs (lavender, basil, thyme, roses, etc.)
¼ cup grated Parmesan cheese
¼ cup pinenuts (optional)
fresh flowers for garnish

   Precook pasta and drain. In separate pan, sauté chicken in olive oil; add shallots
and salt and pepper to taste. Add chicken stock and red peppers and reduce by half.
Add cream and continue to cook until thick and creamy. Add pasta, flowers, and
herbs and warm through. Sprinkle with Parmesan cheese and pinenuts.
   Serve with garnish of fresh flowers.

   Serves 2.

*Longfellow Cafe's chef, Peter Barnard, features delicious pasta dishes and other
preparations in a Northwest style. Both the Longfellow Cafe and its sister restaurant,
The Rhododendron Cafe on Chuckanut Drive in Bow, are owned by Don Shank, and
both take advantage of the Skagit Valley's fresh produce and seafood.*

CREDIT CARDS: V, MC; WHEELCHAIR ACCESS; NON-SMOKING; BEER/WINE; RHODODENDRON
RESERVATIONS FOR FIVE OR MORE

120 North First Street • (206) 336-3684

A JAYS

SEATTLE

POTATO PANCAKES (LATKES)

4-5 large potatoes
1½ medium onions
4 eggs
½ cup matzo meal
½ teaspoon salt
oil

Peel and grate potatoes. Peel onions, cut in quarters, and grate. (Use food processor for grating.) Beat eggs and mix in potatoes, onions, matzo meal and salt. (If mixture is too thin, add more matzo meal; if mixture is too thick, add another egg.)

To cook, place ¼-inch oil in skillet and heat over medium heat to 375°. Drop mixture into hot oil by ¼-cup amounts. Spread to flatten like a pancake. Fry until crisp and golden brown on both sides, about 2-3 minutes per side.

Serve with sour cream or applesauce.

Variations: Add chopped pecans and/or apples to batter.

Makes 16 pancakes.

Imagine the scene: a full house, conversations of the city, the hustle of an urban eatery. Your choices are endless—award-winning pancakes, New York style sandwiches, blintzes, lox and bagels. Owned and operated by Alan Rugoff, A Jay's is one of the most popular spots for breakfast and lunch in Seattle.

CREDIT CARDS: V, MC, AE; WHEELCHAIR ACCESS; SMOKING/NON-SMOKING SECTIONS; NO RESERVATIONS

2619 First Avenue • (206) 441-1511

LE PETIT CAFE

SEATTLE

LE LAPEREAU A'LA DIJONAISE

1 medium, young rabbit, cut in serving pieces
1 tablespoon butter
salt, pepper to taste
1 cup chicken stock
¼ cup lemon juice
¼ cup white wine
½ cup heavy cream
2 tablespoons French mustard
watercress

In a shallow, oven-proof pan, sauté rabbit pieces in butter, seasoning with salt and pepper. When rabbit is nicely brown, remove from pan and set aside on platter. Keep warm.

Add stock, lemon juice, wine and cream to pan. Stir in mustard. Cook until sauce is reduced by half. Add rabbit to sauce. (The sauce will become smooth by itself.) Remove rabbit from pan. Arrange on a shallow platter and surround with sauce. Garnish with watercress.

Serves 4.

Le Petit Cafe has an atmosphere both warm and welcoming. With furnishings of French Country antiques, there is a feeling of elegance; yet ease and comfort are the true hallmarks here. Le Petit has recently celebrated its tenth year and has been acclaimed by critics as one of Seattle's best restaurants. Le Petit is well known for its duck in a raspcherry sauce, scallops in champagne sauce, and chicken in mustard sauce—as well as its light Northwest seafood. Its specialty, however, is homemade lamb sausage served with couscous. Veal and lamb dishes are also featured, as well as homemade desserts.

CREDIT CARDS: V, MC, AE; WHEELCHAIR ACCESS; BEER/WINE; RESERVATIONS
3428 Northeast Fifty-fifth Street • (206) 524-0819

THE PINK DOOR

SEATTLE

INSALATA DI MARE

3 lbs. small clams
2 lbs. mussels
white wine
1 lb. squid, cleaned and sliced in rounds, including tentacles
bay leaf
black peppercorns
12-16 medium sized prawns, peeled and deveined
1½ cups finely chopped parsley
¼ teaspoon celery salt
salt and white pepper to taste
2 cups extra virgin olive oil
1 large onion, chopped medium
6 stalks celery, sliced in medium-sized pieces
4-6 lemon wedges
lettuce leaves

Steam clams and mussels in separate pans with enough water and a splash of white wine to cover bottom of pan. Remove with slotted spoon as soon as they open. Drain very well.

Simmer squid for 5 minutes in water to cover, which has been seasoned with a bay leaf and a few peppercorns. Drain well and remove bay leaf and peppercorns.

Simmer prawns, barely covered in water, for 2 minutes. Drain.

Combine lemon juice, parsley, celery salt, salt and white pepper in a large bowl. Slowly whisk in olive oil. Stir in onion, celery and all the seafood. Marinate for at least 1 hour, stirring once or twice. Before serving, bring to room temperature for 15 minutes. Toss well and serve with a lemon wedge on a bed of green leaf lettuce. Buon Appetito!

Serves 4 to 6.

Suggested wine: Pinot Grigio

Jackie Robert's Italian eatery has a flair for fun and dining that's as delicious as it is entertaining. Approached via Post Alley in the historic Pike Place Market, this unique restaurant is marked only by its famous pink door—no sign. A cozy candlelit dining room, recently joined by a bar and cabaret room, never fails to delight patrons. During the summer an outdoor deck overlooking the Puget Sound is filled with happy patrons who keep returning for food which is inspired with love and a sincere wish to please.

CREDIT CARDS: V, MC; SMOKING/NON-SMOKING SECTIONS; FULL BAR; RESERVATIONS SUGGESTED

1919 Post Alley • (206) 443-3241

SALEH AL LAGO

SEATTLE

STUFFED LAMB RIB-EYES

3 tablespoons cream cheese
2 tablespoons mushrooms, finely chopped
dash of brandy
few mint leaves, chopped
salt and pepper to taste
6-8 spinach leaves, washed and dried
6-8 slices prosciutto
thinly sliced avocado
2 10 oz. boneless lamb rib eyes*, slit lengthwise through center, leaving in one piece
¼ cup red wine
2 cups veal or lamb stock
1 tablespoon butter

Soften cream cheese; mix with mushrooms, brandy and mint. Adjust salt and pepper to taste. Lay out spinach leaves, overlapping each other, making 2 cradles for the stuffing. Place a layer of prosciutto atop each spinach bed. Then spread the cream cheese mixture over this. Arrange slices of avocado down center, lengthwise. Roll the spinach, lengthwise, around the stuffing. Refrigerate to firm up.

Gently press the stuffing into the slit of the lamb. Close lamb around the stuffing. Secure opening with a toothpick to tie closed. In a sauté pan, brown the roasts in a little oil. Transfer to roasting pan. Bake in a 350° oven for about 10-15 minutes, or to desired doneness. Keep warm while preparing sauce.

To prepare sauce, drain oil from the pan used for browning the roasts. Pour in the drippings from the roasting pan. Over medium-high heat, add the red wine. Reduce by one-third. Add the stock and reduce to ½ cup. Lower heat to medium-low. Add butter. Stir to thicken. Adjust seasoning. Pour sauce onto plate and arrange sliced lamb over it.

Serves 4.

* The rib-eye is the meaty portion of the rack (rib). Ask butcher to bone it out.

Since its opening in 1982, Saleh al Lago has received accolades both locally and nationally for its central Italian cuisine, its elegant design and its beautiful view of Greenlake. Saleh Joudeh, the owner and chef, prepares dishes to order with consummate skill in an open kitchen using the highest quality ingredients, including beef and veal tenderloin, fresh seafood, and pasta made right in the restaurant.

CREDIT CARDS: V, MC, AE, CB, DC; WHEELCHAIR ACCESS; SMOKING/NON-SMOKING SECTIONS; FULL BAR; RESERVATIONS REQUIRED

6804 East Greenlake Way North • (206) 524-4044

THE ONION

BBQ BABY BACK RIBS

8 1¾ to 2¼ lbs. baby back pork loin ribs

Boiling Mixture:

2 gallons water	1 lb. celery
2 lb. onion	2 cups cooking Burgundy wine

Barbecue Sauce:

6 oz. green pepper (about 1 cup chopped)	½ cup mustard
6 oz. onion (about 1⅓ cups, chopped)	1 tablespoon Tobasco sauce
½ cup water	½ teaspoon liquid smoke
3 cups brown sugar	1 tablespoon Worcestershire sauce
2 cups molasses	4 cups Kraft barbecue sauce
	3¼ cups ketchup

Cut onions and celery into 1-inch chunks. Put whole racks of ribs into a large pot and cover with water. Add the onion, celery and Burgundy. Bring to a boil and simmer for 1½-2 hours or until meat is tender and pulls easily away from the bones. Add water as necessary to keep ribs covered.

Chop green pepper and onion and run through blender with the water until smooth. Add all other ingredients; stir and simmer for 45 minutes.

When ribs are tender, drain and remove from pot to dry. When BBQ sauce has simmered, remove from heat to cool. Both items may be made in advance and refrigerated until needed.

Dip whole rib rack into BBQ sauce or paint on with brush. Place on barbecue broiler or in broiler pan. Broil, turning every few minutes, until ribs are glazed and appear candied.

Place cooked rib rack on cutting board. To facilitate eating, cut between the bones two-thirds of the way from the bottom towards the top of the rack.

Serve entire rack on a plate with a side of BBQ sauce for dipping.

8 servings.

Note: Recipe can easily be halved.

Fun, friendly and fast characterize The Onion. The original antique back bar helps create the fabulous "Chicago Saloon" atmosphere at this popular downtown spot. The real source of The Onion's popularity, however, is its food: BBQ Baby Back Pork Ribs, sizzling fajitas, chicken platters, fettucine, and gourmet salads. "But don't forget we're famous for our hamburgers," says genial owner Larry Brown. His Northgate Onion, at 7522 N. Division, promises the same exciting fare and festivity.

CREDIT CARDS: V, MC, AE, DC, DISC; WHEELCHAIR ACCESS; SMOKING/NON-SMOKING SECTIONS; FULL BAR; NO RESERVATIONS

302 West Riverside • (509) 483-2161

EZELL'S SWEET POTATO PIE

1 lb. yams (about 3 cups sliced)
2½ tablespoons butter
½ cup sugar
½ cup plus 1 tablespoon milk
1 egg yolk
½ teaspoon cinnamon
¾ teaspoon nutmeg
8-inch pie crust (see recipe below)

Makes an 8-inch pie.

Peel yams. Cut into ¼-inch slices. Put potatoes in a saucepan with enough water to cover by at least 1 inch. Bring to boil. Reduce heat to medium-high; continue low boiling for 15 minutes or until tender. Drain. Put hot yams in mixing bowl. With an electric mixer, beat in butter, mixing until melted. Add remaining ingredients except crust, beating well after each ingredient. Pour into pie crust. Bake in a preheated oven at 350° for 1 hour.

Pie Crust: Place 1 cup flour and ½ teaspoon salt in bowl. Cut in ⅓ cup shortening. Sprinkle with 2-3 tablespoons water. Mix just until dough forms a ball. Shape dough into a flat round on a flour-covered board. Roll dough into a 10-inch circle. Fit into an 8-inch pie pan. Trim or flute edges.

Ezell's Fried Chicken is a family owned restaurant serving some of the freshest and best food in the nation. The restaurant does catering, and delivery is available. Ezell's presently has two locations to serve its loyal patrons.

NO CREDIT CARDS; WHEELCHAIR ACCESS; NO RESERVATIONS
501 - 23rd Ave • (206) 324-4141 • 4216 University Way NE • (206) 548-1455

ROSLYN CAFE

BAVARIAN SCRAMBLE

4 medium red potatoes
3 tablespoons margarine
½ cup diced yellow onion
1 tomato, diced
½ teaspoon caraway seed
8 eggs, beaten well
¾ cup grated Cheddar cheese
salt, pepper to taste
8 of your favorite Polish sausages (about 1 lb. total)
½ cup sour cream

Precook red potatoes by boiling until tender; cool, then quarter and slice thin. Brown potatoes over medium-high heat in frying pan with 2 tablespoons margarine. Mix in onions, tomatoes and caraway seed. Pour eggs into pan, stirring often. Before totally set up, add cheddar cheese and melt in thoroughly. Season with salt and pepper. At same time as eggs are cooking, heat 1 tablespoon margarine in another frying pan. Fry Polish sausage, sliced in half lengthwise, until heated. When serving, top egg scramble with dollop of sour cream with sausage on the side. Serve with sourdough toast, biscuits or muffins, and fresh fruit.

Serves 4.

Roslyn Cafe offers hearty breakfasts, gourmet burgers, steak sandwiches on freshly baked buns, and also elegant dinners with ever-changing specials. The atmosphere is relaxed in Roslyn and Kim Jury's menu successfully appeals to the varied tastes of a great array of visitors to this historic coal-mining community. Freshly baked cakes, pies and cobblers make choosing a dessert difficult; but any choice will be a perfect ending for a meal at the Roslyn Cafe.

CREDIT CARDS: V, MC; FULL BAR; NO RESERVATIONS
Second and Pennsylvania • (509) 649-2763

MAMOUNIA
MOROCCAN RESTAURANT

SEATTLE

CHICKEN WITH LEMON

2 Cornish hens
1 bunch parsley
1 bunch cilantro
2 medium-sized onions
1 teaspoons salt
1 teaspoon white pepper
1 teaspoon ground coriander
1 teaspoon ginger
1 teaspoon saffron or yellow coloring
1 cup olive oil
1 marinated lemon (see preparation below)

Chop parsley and cilantro; mince onion. Place in large, oven-proof pot. Add salt, pepper, coriander, ginger, saffron and oil. Place hens in pot on their sides. Fill with enough water to reach half-way up hens. Bake at 350° degrees for 45-60 minutes or until done. Watch carefully, turning hens occasionally.

To serve, pour sauce from pot over hens and garnish with marinated lemon slices.

Preparation of marinated lemons: cut lemons into quarters, leaving 1 inch uncut at bottom, in order to hold it together. Place in a marinade of 1 gallon water, ½ cup vinegar and 1 cup salt. Let stand 2 weeks or longer.

Serves 4.

As guests become accustomed to the dimly lit interior of the Mamounia Moroccan Restaurant, they feel they are inside a tent. Diners recline on a velvet banquette which encircles the room, or on floor cushions. In a room filled with the tantalizing aromas of Mid-eastern dishes, attentive waiters in authentic Moroccan costume assist patrons in the selection of their meal. A five-course dinner, served on low tables of carved wood and ending with the washing of hands in rose water, is truly a cultural experience.

CREDIT CARDS: V, MC, AE; WHEELCHAIR ACCESS; BEER/WINE; RESERVATIONS REQUIRED ON WEEKENDS

1556 East Olive Way • (206) 329-3886

L'APERO
SEATTLE

RED SNAPPER WITH SAFFRON SAUCE

2 tablespoons butter
1 tablespoon chopped shallots
1 cup dry white wine
pinch of Spanish saffron
¼ cup clam juice
¾ cup whipping cream
16 Penn Cove mussels
4 red snapper fillets (6-8 oz. each)
olive oil
2 tablespoons chopped chives

In a sauté pan, melt 1 tablespoon butter. Add shallots, white wine, saffron and clam juice. Cook until reduced by half. Add cream; boil 2-3 minutes longer. Add mussels and 1 tablespoon butter. Cook just until mussels open.

Meanwhile, broil or sauté fish in a little olive oil until cooked as desired. To serve, pour sauce with mussels over fish and sprinkle with chopped chives.

Serves 4.

L'Apero, a delightful little bistro in Madison Park, radiates European ambience. The owner-chef, Guillaume Bonzon, prepares dishes with a Mediterranean flavor. The menu offers a selection of mesquite-broiled fresh fish and several steak preparations with a variety of sauces. Also on the menu are shellfish, chicken and veal specialties and an interesting selection of salads.

CREDIT CARDS: V, MC; WHEELCHAIR ACCESS; SMOKING/NON-SMOKING SECTIONS; BEER/WINE; RESERVATIONS ACCEPTED

4220 East Madison • (206) 324-4140

MEDITERRANEAN
KITCHEN

BABA KHANOUJ

1 medium-sized eggplant (about 1 lb.)
¼ cup fresh lemon juice
2 large cloves garlic, crushed
5 tablespoons tahini (sesame seed paste)
olive oil
cubes of cucumber and tomato
pita bread

Broil eggplant over gas flame for 10-15 minutes until very soft and dark. Peel eggplant and mash to a smooth purée. Mix in lemon juice, garlic and tahini. Spread on a serving plate. Sprinkle top with olive oil. Garnish with cucumbers and tomatoes. Serve as a spread or dip for pita bread.

Makes 1½ cups.

In very few restaurants can one find the ethnic variety of entrees that are found in the Mediterranean Kitchen. North African, Israeli, Iraqi—most cultures in the Mediterrean basin are represented on the menu of this charming and authentic restaurant. The credit for the Mediterrean Kitchen's success goes to its chef Kamal Aboul Hosn, known for his salads and couscous.

CREDIT CARDS: V, MC, AE, DC; WHEELCHAIR ACCESS; SMOKING/NON-SMOKING SECTIONS; BEER/WINE; RESERVATIONS REQUIRED

Four West Roy • (206) 285-6713

NIKKO RESTAURANT   SEATTLE

SOLE KARAAGE

4 rex sole (available at fish markets, cleaned, skinned and head removed)
oil for deep frying
salt
flour
sauce (see below)

Fillet the fish. Soak bones in salt water (sea water) for 30-40 minutes. Drain and let dry completely in a food dehydrator or in oven at lowest temperature. (This takes about 8-10 hours in oven.)

Deep-fry bones in hot (360°) oil for about 15-20 minutes or until crunchy. Salt fillets lightly and dredge in flour. Deep-fry until crisp.

To serve, accompany any fish fillets and bones with sauce for dipping.

Sauce: combine ponsu sauce (Japanese fruit vinegar) with grated white radish, chili pepper and soy sauce to taste.

Serves 4.

Nikko has been proclaimed by discerning diners and critics to be Seattle's best and most popular sushi bar. Owner-chef Shiro Kashiba serves outstanding traditional Japanese food as well as unique and exquisite specialties of his own.

CREDIT CARDS: V, MC, AE, DC; FULL BAR; RESERVATIONS REQUIRED
1306 South King Street • (206) 322-4905

WINSTON'S BREAD

2½ cups hot water (about 100°)
½ cup sugar
1 tablespoon salt
3 (¼ oz.) packets dry yeast
½ cup oil
6-7 cups bread flour
melted butter

Combine 1¼ cups water, ¼ cup sugar, 1½ teaspoons salt, and yeast in a small bowl. Let stand 5-7 minutes, or until doubled.

In a large bowl, mix together remaining 1¼ cups water, ¼ cup sugar, 1½ teaspoons salt, and oil. Stir in yeast mixture. Beat in 3 cups flour on high speed of electric mixer, adding flour, 1 cup at a time. Beat until a thick batter forms. Let stand in a warm location until batter has doubled in size, about 20 minutes.

With a wooden spoon, mix in 3 cups flour until dough forms. Turn out on floured board and knead in an additional ½-1 cup flour. Knead until smooth and elastic. Oil a large bowl and add dough. Cover with a damp, warm cloth and set aside in a warm location until doubled in size.

Divide dough into thirds. Shape each portion into a loaf. Place in greased loaf pans. Cover and set in a warm location until doubled in size.

Bake in a preheated oven at 350° for 20 minutes. Baste tops of loaves with melted butter, Bake 10 minutes and baste again. Bake 5-10 minutes longer or until loaves are golden brown.

Makes 3 loaves.

Winston's offers its guests a variety of entrees from poultry to the freshest seafood in the islands. Critics have not only praised Winston's for its exquisitely prepared food but for its unique historical setting—the Sears Kit Home built in the early 1900's. Winston's truly provides an elegant dining experience with a personal flair.

CREDIT CARDS: V, MC; WHEELCHAIR ACCESS; SMOKING; BEER/WINE; RESERVATIONS REQUIRED ON WEEKENDS

95 Nichols Street • (206) 378-5093

THE GREYSTONE RESTAURANT

YAKIMA

THE GREYSTONE'S STUFFED BREAST OF CHICKEN

1 oz. each Hungarian, Italian and German sausage
1 medium apple, finely chopped
¼ cup onion, finely chopped
1 tablespoon butter
1 cup Yakima Valley Gouda cheese, finely grated
1 cup Parmesan cheese, finely grated
¼ cup sour cream
4 oz. cream cheese, softened and cut in small pieces
¾ cup chopped parsley
¾ cup finely ground bread crumbs
1 teaspoon nutmeg
½ teaspoon salt
½ teaspoon white pepper
6-8 boned and skinned chicken breast
fresh spinach leaves, steamed
brandy sauce (see below)

Cut sausage in ½-inch slices and steam in a small amount of water for 5 minutes. Drain and finely chop. Combine with apple and onion and sauté in butter. Mix together remaining ingredients, except chicken, spinach and brandy sauce. Stir in sausage mixture. Pound each breast and place a spinach leaf on each. Spoon about 3-4 tablespoons of stuffing mixture on each breast.* Roll up and secure with a skewer. Baste with melted, seasoned butter. Bake, covered, in a 350° oven for 20 minutes, or until done. Baste 2-4 more times while baking.

To serve, slice each breast, fan out, and serve with brandy sauce.

Brandy sauce: reduce 1 quart homemade chicken stock (very strong) to one-third. Stir in 1-2 ounces brandy. Cook on high heat for about 5 minutes. Take off heat. Slowly stir in 2-3 ounces homemade crème fraîche. Season with salt, pepper and lemon juice.

* Any leftover filling may be frozen, used as a spread for melba toast, or used as a filling for filo dough appetizers.

Serves 6-8.

In the fall of 1983, a dream of twelve years came true for Gayla Games-Hopkins and Nancy Beveridge—The Greystone Restaurant. With the skills of chef Steven Wood, who received his culinary training from Seattle Community College, and the skills of Manager Annie Megofma, The Greystone Restaurant offers its guests the freshness of Northwest foods, a wine list specializing in Northwest wines, and a menu that rotates with the seasons. Gayla and Nancy have created a truly fine dining experience with an atmosphere that is friendly and casual, but with an ambience reminiscent of the turn of the century.

CREDIT CARDS: V, MC, AE; WHEELCHAIR ACCESS; SMOKING/NON-SMOKING; FULL BAR; RESERVATIONS RECOMMENDED

5 North Front Street • (509) 248-9801

THE HERBFARM   FALL CITY

SORBET OF LAVENDER AND VIOLETS

This remarkable sorbet is both flavored and colored by two edible flowers. Because of the floral-perfumy bouquet, the nose fools the tastebuds into thinking the sorbet is really sweeter than it is.

At the Herbfarm — where luncheons run 6 courses and dinners up to 9 — we serve this sorbet in the summer between courses as a luxurious palate refresher. Try pairing it with apple slices, pear, and quince.

1⅔ cups water
11 tablespoons sugar
25 lavender flower heads
8 violets or pansies
2 tablespoons lime juice

Prepare the sugar syrup: Combine about three-fourths of the sugar with three-fourths of the water. Bring the mixture to a boil and allow it to cool to room temperature.

Prepare the lavender flowers: Pluck the individual flowers from the English lavender stems. This is necessary because the stems would otherwise discolor the final sorbet.

Put the lavender flowers (reserve the violets) into a food processor fitted with the metal blade. Add the remaining quarter of the sugar. Whirl about 3 minutes — until the flowers are completely integrated into the sugar.

Dissolve the lavender flower sugar: Add the lavender flower purée to the cooled sugar syrup. Stir. Let the mixture stand at room temperature for at least 1 hour. Strain through a fine sieve.

Steep the violets: Take remaining water and bring to a bare boil. Turn off heat. Add violets and let steep 10 minutes. Stir and squeeze to release the blue coloring. Strain out flowers.

Combine and freeze: Combine the lavender and violet infusions. Freeze in an ice cream machine according to manufacturer's instructions. Alternately, put mixture in a metal bowl in the freezer. Scrape down the sides every hour or so until frozen. Serve in a chilled wine glass and garnish with a violet.

Serves 8.

"How better to approach our culinary roots than with a restaurant right on a farm," say *Ron Zimmerman and Carrie Van Dyck, owners of The Herbfarm. With a large kitchen garden just steps from the dining room, they select the best from the farm and wilds to create luncheons with flavors of the region and season. Chef Ron Zimmerman orchestrates unique six-course prix fixe luncheons and up to nine-course theme dinners from April through Christmas each year.*

CREDIT CARDS: V, MC; WHEELCHAIR ACCESS; NON-SMOKING; BEER/WINE; RESERVATIONS REQUIRED

32804 Issaquah-Fall City Road • (206) 784-2222

SALAL CAFE

PORT TOWNSEND

TOFU STROGANOFF

¼ cup garlic butter
1 cup thinly sliced mushrooms
¾ cup broccoli florets
1-1½ cups cubed, marinated firm tofu*
¼ cup sour cream
½ cup whipping cream
1 teaspoon basil
¼ cup white wine
4 cups cooked (al dente) homemade pasta
¼ cup grated Parmesan cheese

Sauté tofu cubes, broccoli, and mushrooms in garlic butter until broccoli is bright green but still a little crisp. Add basil and white wine and stir. Add sour cream and cream; stir until smooth. Add ¼ cup Parmesan, then the cooked pasta. Toss lightly until pasta is hot. Garnish with remaining Parmesan and dash of paprika.

Serve with tossed fresh salad** and sourdough garlic toast.

* Our tofu is Soy Deli (Quon Hop) firm, vacuum packed. This is the only brand we've found that's firm enough to retain its shape and provide a chewy texture. Our marinade is made by the gallon as follows: 2 cups cider vinegar,1½ cups lemon juice, ¼ cup honey. Then fill jar with Tamari soy sauce. Tofu is cut into ½-inch slices, covered with marinade and finely-minced fresh garlic and ginger, marinated overnight, then drained on paper towels and cubed.

** Our green salad is a mixture of hand-torn Romaine and green leaf lettuce, sliced red cabbage, and grated carrot, topped with florets of cauliflower and broccoli, cucumber, radish, red onion slices, tomato wedges, sweet red pepper strips, and alfalfa sprouts, and served with one of our homemade salad dressings on the side (Italian, Italian-bleu cheese, creamy bleu cheese, yogurt or dill).

Serves 4.

The Salal Cafe features a wide range of American cuisine with the emphasis on quality. Popular since 1982 for its outstanding breakfasts and lunches, the Salal has recently begun serving dinners of the same fine quality much to the delight of its many afficionados. The restaurant is cooperatively owned and managed, a fact that certainly contributes to the friendly attentiveness one receives.

CREDIT CARDS: V, MC; WHEELCHAIR ACCESS (NOT TO RESTROOMS); SMOKING/NON-SMOKING SECTIONS; BEER/WINE; NO RESERVATIONS, BREAKFAST, LUNCH; RESERVATIONS RECOMMENDED, DINNER

634 Water Street • (206) 385-6532

RISTORANTE PONY

LEG OF LAMB WITH CUMIN AND FIGS

10 oz. boneless leg of lamb, cut in 1-inch cubes
salt and pepper to taste
1 teaspoon cumin
4 red new potatoes, quartered and parboiled (unpeeled)
1 tablespoon olive oil
2 tablespoons butter
1 tablespoon minced garlic and/or shallots
⅓ cup sliced red and yellow peppers
½ cup dry red wine
½ cup lamb stock
6 medium fresh figs, halved
green onions or parsley

    Season lamb with salt, pepper and cumin. Brown lamb and potatoes in olive oil; then remove from pan. Add 1 tablespoon butter, and sauté garlic and peppers. Add wine and stock, and reduce by one-third. Add lamb, potatoes and figs, and cook lamb until medium rare. Stir in remaining butter to thicken; garnish with green onion or parsley.

Lois Pierris originally opened the Ristorante Pony in 1978 as a coffee house. Over the years it has grown into a small, intimate, full service restaurant with a distinctive European flavor. The restaurant is known for its wonderfully prepared Mediterranean dishes as well as its selection of wines and liquors from all around the world. The finale, however, to a fine meal at Ristorante Pony is one of the desserts created by Lois Pierris.

CREDIT CARDS: V, MC; FULL BAR

621½ Queen Anne Avenue North • (206) 283-8658

EVERGREEN RESTAURANT   EDMONDS

SHRIMP, SCALLOP AND CHICKEN COMBINATION

4 dried mushrooms
1 green pepper
1 red pepper
1 whole chicken breast or 2 thighs
15 shrimp (#25-30), peeled
10 scallops
1 egg white
3½ teaspoons cornstarch
¾ teaspoon salt
1 tablespoon dry sherry
1 teaspoon water
1 teaspoon sesame oil
⅛ teaspoon white pepper
½ cup vegetable oil
½ green onion, cut into ¼-inch pieces
½ cup sliced bamboo shoots
10 snow peas
½ cup sliced water chestnuts

Wash dried mushrooms and soak in warm water for at least 30 minutes. Dice into ½-inch squares. Dice peppers into ½-inch squares. Debone chicken and slice into ½-inch squares. Slice each shrimp in half lengthwise. Combine chicken, scallops, and shrimp with egg white, 3 teaspoons of the cornstarch, ¼ teaspoon of the salt, and sherry. Let marinate for 20 minutes. Combine water, ½ teaspoon of the salt, ½ teaspoon of the cornstarch, sesame oil and white pepper in a small bowl; set aside.

Heat vegetable oil in a wok to medium-high or about 350°. Stir-fry chicken, scallops and shrimp until chicken turns white. Remove from wok and drain oil. Reheat 2 tablespoons of the oil until it is very hot. Add green onion and stir-fry for a few seconds; add mushrooms and bamboo shoots, and stir-fry for 1 minute. Add green and red peppers, snow peas and water chestnuts and stir well. Mix in chicken, scallops, shrimp and sauce mixture. Cook until sauce thickens.

Serves 4.

At The Evergreen owners Nai-Hsi Wu and Brian Ma have established gourmet standards of culinary quality and service, incorporating harmonious color, attractive fragrance and tantalizing taste. They take great pride in the abilities of chefs Shu-Huai Kong and Zhe-Huang Tsai, who create authentic Szechwan, Hunan and Mandarin Chinese cuisine.

CREDIT CARDS: V, MC; SMOKING/NON-SMOKING; FULL BAR

23628 Highway 99 • (206) 771-8874

142

UNION BAY CAFE
SEATTLE
BUCKWHEAT CREPES WITH SMOKED DUCK

Crepes:

3 eggs, beaten
1 cup water
1 cup milk
½ teaspoon salt
3 tablespoons melted butter
½ cup buckwheat flour
⅔ cup all-purpose flour

Sauce:

2 tablespoons chopped shallots
2 tablespoons butter
2 oz. sliced mushrooms
2 teaspoons raspberry vinegar
¼ cup dry Marsala

Filling:

2 medium onions, sliced
2 tablespoons butter
salt, pepper
2 teaspoons raspberry vinegar
1 lb. mushrooms, sliced
1 whole smoked duckling, boned and meat
   thinly julienned*

½ cup veal stock (chicken stock may
   be substituted)
1 cup cream
salt, pepper, and lemon juice to taste

Garnish: **Diced apple, pomegranate seeds or red bell pepper, and scallions**

To prepare crepes, beat together eggs, water, milk, salt and butter. Whisk flours in quickly. Strain and let sit at least ½ hour. (May be made ahead.) Over medium-low heat, prepare crepes, using about 3 tablespoons batter per crepe. Makes approximately 18 8-inch crepes. Set aside.

To prepare filling, sauté onions in 1 tablespoon butter over medium heat, stirring frequently, until browned and sweet. Season with salt and pepper to taste. Add 1 teaspoon vinegar and cook briefly. Set aside. Sauté mushrooms in remaining tablespoon of butter. Season with salt and pepper to taste. Add remaining teaspoon of vinegar and cook briefly. Mix with onions and combine with the smoked duckling meat. Place 2 tablespoons filling on one quarter of crepe and fold twice. May be covered and refrigerated overnight.

To prepare sauce, lightly brown shallots in butter. Add mushrooms and sauté briefly. Add vinegar and reduce by two-thirds. Add Marsala and reduce by one-half. Stir in stock and reduce by one-half. Add cream and reduce until sauce is lightly thickened. Season with salt, pepper and lemon juice to taste.

To serve, place filled crepes on lightly buttered sheet pan and heat through in a 400° oven. Top with sauce and garnish with apple, pomegranate seeds and scallions.

* available at Seattle Super Smoke

Appetizers for 12 or light dinner for 6.

Wine suggestion: any full-bodied red champagne

Starting with a love for the foods of Italy and the Mediterranean, owner-chef Mark Manley creates a very personal cuisine using skills finely honed in some of Seattle's and Chicago's finest kitchens. His enthusiastic patrons enjoy the casually elegant atmosphere and the changing array of works of some of the Northwest's foremost contemporary artists. But most of all they enjoy Mark's culinary artistry.

CREDIT CARDS: V, MC; WHEELCHAIR ACCESS; NON-SMOKING; BEER/WINE; RESERVATIONS ACCEPTED

3505 Northeast Forty-fifth • (206) 527-8364

PATSY CLARK'S MANSION
SPOKANE
CURRIED CASHEW CHICKEN

4 boneless chicken breasts, dredged in flour
¼ cup clarified butter
¼ cup mango chutney, finely chopped
¼ cup sherry
2 tablespoons curry powder
1½ cups cream
½ cup whole cashews

Sauté chicken in a little clarified butter until two-thirds cooked. Add remaining ingredients except cashews. Let ingredients reduce, with chicken, until sauce is thick and creamy. Before serving add cashews.

Patsy Clark's Mansion is one of the oldest mansions in the Northwest. It is unique in that it has retained most of its original furnishings, beautifully displayed for all visitors of the mansion to see. Chef Kirstie Boulanger offers only the finest food, accompanied by equally superior liquors and wines, just as Patrick "Patsy" Clark did from 1898 to 1915.

CREDIT CARDS: V, MC, AE, DC; SMOKING/NON-SMOKING SECTIONS; FULL BAR; RESERVATIONS SUGGESTED

West 2208 Second Avenue • (509) 838-8300

SANCTUARY RESTAURANT   CHINOOK

CHINOOK SALMON POACHED

four 6 oz. salmon fillets
salt and pepper to taste
twelve mussels (optional)
pinch of saffron
4 minced shallots
¾ cup tomatoes, chopped fine

½ cup sherry wine
1½ cup clams juice
1 tablespoon unsalted butter
juice of 1 lemon
1 tablespoon cornstarch
deep-fried celery leaves (see recipe below)

Place salmon in deep-sided fry pan just large enough to hold the salmon in one layer. Sprinkle with salt and pepper to taste, pinch of saffron, shallots and tomatoes. Pour the wine and clam juice over the salmon; bring to a boil over moderate heat. Turn heat down and poach the salmon covered with a lid or foil, turning once after 10 minutes. Add the mussels and poach for an additional 3-5 minutes until salmon flakes and mussels are open. Transfer mussels and salmon to a platter and keep warm. Combine lemon juice and cornstarch; add to the poaching liquid and boil until reduced to about 1 cup. Stir in butter. Adjust seasonings if necessary. Strain sauce and pour over salmon. Top with the deep-fried celery leaves. Garnish entree with the mussels. Serve with sliced cooked red potatoes and your favorite green salad topped with pinenuts.

Deep-fried Celery Leaves:

½ cup pale ale or club soda
⅓ cup flour
¼ teaspoon salt
1 cup celery leaves
vegetable oil

Whisk together ale, flour and salt until smooth. Dust wet celery leaves lightly with flour. Dip in ale batter. Fry in about 2 inches of hot oil (375°) until pale in color, turning once. Drain on paper towels and keep warm.

Serves 4.

Suggested wine: 1986 Waterbrook Chardonnay

The Sanctuary is located in a turn-of-the-century church building, complete with stained glass windows. Owners Joanne and Geno Leech provide a relaxed, friendly atmosphere. Veteran chef Fernand Lopez expertly prepares fresh local seafood from a lower Columbia cannery a few blocks from the restaurant, and Joanne's creative desserts complement the well-rounded menu. The chocolate rum cake and the zesty lemon cream sherbert are simply divine.

CREDIT CARDS: V, MC AE; WHEELCHAIR ACCESS; FULL BAR; RESERVATIONS SUGGESTED
Highway 101 and Hazel Street • (206) 777-8380

ROANOKE EXIT RESTAURANT

SEATTLE

PAN FRIED OYSTERS

Breaded Oysters and Fennel:

¼ cup flour
1 egg
1 tablespoon milk
½ cup fine bread crumbs
16 Yearling Pacific oysters, shucked
  and rinsed

¼ cup oil
2 fennel bulbs, cored and sliced thin
lemon zest or lemon wedges

Place flour in small bowl. Beat egg with milk in another bowl. Place bread crumbs in a third bowl. Coat oysters with flour; dip in egg mixture; and then coat with bread crumbs. Set aside.

Heat oil in large skillet over medium to medium-high heat. When hot, but not smoking, sauté fennel until golden brown, stirring frequently. Remove with slotted spoon and place on warm serving platter. Keep warm. Sauté oysters in same skillet over medium heat until golden brown and slightly firm to the touch. Remove and place on top of fennel; garnish with lemon zest or lemon wedges. Offer tarragon mayonnaise in a separate serving dish.

Tarragon Mayonnaise:

2 eggs
1 oz. fresh tarragon, chopped, rinsed,
  and blanched for 30 seconds
1 teaspoon chopped fresh garlic
1 cup olive oil or salad oil

2-4 oz. (4-8 tablespoons) tarragon vinegar
  (to taste)
small amount oyster liquid (optional)
salt and pepper to taste

With food processor on medium speed, blend eggs, tarragon, and garlic. Slowly add oil. Then slowly add tarragon vinegar. Add oyster liquid if desired. Season with salt and pepper. Place mayonnaise in serving bowl and cover. If kept chilled, tarragon mayonnaise may be made a day ahead.

4 appetizer servings.

Roanoke Exit has been an Eastlake tradition since 1981. What keeps the enthusiastic regulars who aren't interested in the "see and be seen" scene coming back is the combination of marvelous food, reasonable prices, a truly comfortable "neighborhood cafe" atmosphere and very personalized service. The credit goes to owner Diane Symms and chef Christopher Kerns, who has a fantastic flair for combining ingredients to produce unusual and tasty fare. Chef Kerns is especially known for his fresh daily seafood specials. Diane Symms also owns The Wild Strawberry in South Seattle, a breakfast and lunch deli, and Lombardi's in Ballard, an Italian restaurant.

CREDIT CARDS: V, MC, AE; WHEELCHAIR ACCESS; SMOKING/NONSMOKING SECTIONS; FULL BAR
2366 Eastlake East • (206) 328-2775

JOHNNY'S

YAKIMA

ROASTED RACK OF LAMB

4 10 oz. racks of lamb
2 teaspoons salt mixed with 1 teaspoon pepper
¾ cup Dijon mustard
4 tablespoons whole rosemary
1½-2 cups course, dry bread crumbs
4 poached pear halves*
mint jelly sauce**

Trim fat cap off tops of lamb racks. Season each rack with ¾ teaspoon salt/pepper mixture. Spread each rack with 3 tablespoons mustard and sprinkle with 1 tablespoon rosemary. Coat racks with bread crumbs. Roast in a 350° oven until lamb reaches 140° on a meat thermometer, about 20-25 minutes.

Garnish each serving of lamb with a fanned pear half and accompany with a small cup of mint jelly sauce.

* Poach peeled and cored pear halves in 4 cups water, ½ cup white wine and 3 tablespoons sugar for 2 minutes. Chill pears until ready to serve.

** Prepare mint jelly sauce by blending ½ cup mint jelly with ¾ cup Hollandaise sauce. Serve at room temperature.

Serves 4.

Johnny's, which opened December of 1987, offers continental cuisine as well as a fresh fish menu daily. It is a gourmet's choice for exceptional dining, including the excitement of table-side preparations of flambé dishes, all done in an atmosphere of marble, copper, etched glass and handsome mahogany.

CREDIT CARDS: V, MC, AE, CB, DC, DISC.; WHEELCHAIR ACCESS; FULL BAR; RESERVATIONS SUGGESTED

Towne Plaza, North Seventh Street and Yakima Avenue • (509) 248-5900

THE LOBSTER
SHOP AT DASH POINT
TACOMA

CIOPPINO AND PORTUGUESE LOBSTER POT

cioppino base (see recipe below)
½ lb. salmon, cut in chunks
½ lb. white fish, cut in chunks
½ lb. King crab (in the shell)
8 prawns (21-25 ct.)
3 dozen mussels
3 dozen clams
½ lb. bay shrimp
four 5 oz. lobster tails, split, with other seafood

Prepare base as directed. Refrigerate, covered, for 1-3 days, allowing flavors to blend.

When ready to serve, bring base to boil in a large pot. Add all seafood except bay shrimp. Reduce heat and simmer until seafood is cooked, adding bay shrimp during last few minutes. Serve in bowls.

Note: Any combination of seafood can be used in this recipe, depending on your preference and what is in season.

Cioppino Base:

1 large onion, cut in ½-inch chunks
1 lb. carrots, cut in attractive, bite-sized pieces
2 (15 oz.) cans tomato sauce
1 (28 oz.) can crushed tomatoes in purée
1 (4 oz.) can chopped green chilies
2-3 large cloves garlic, minced

1½ teaspoons dried thyme
¾ teaspoon dried rosemary, crushed
1 tablespoon dried basil
1½ teaspoons coarse-ground pepper
2 cups water
1 cup red wine

Steam onion and carrots until tender. Add to remaining ingredients in a large pot. Bring to boil. Simmer 2 hours, uncovered. Thin with a little water or red wine if necessary.

Serves 6-8.

The Dash Point Lobster Shop's unique beach setting and its cozy out-of-the-way charm, combined with an exciting and extensive seafood menu, make this the perfect place for celebrating special days—or for turning any day into a special day. Their newer location on Rustin Way in Tacoma will work the same magic.

CREDIT CARDS: V, MC, AE, CB, DC, DISC; BEER/WINE; RESERVATIONS REQUIRED
6912 Soundview Drive Northeast • (206) 927-1513

MORELAND'S
RESTAURANT

SPOKANE

PHEASANT WITH CHARDONNAY-CHOCOLATE SAUCE

Roast Pheasant:

1 2-3 lb. pheasant
1 teaspoon salt
½ teaspoon freshly ground black pepper
1 teaspoon dried thyme leaves

½ cup (1 stick) unsalted butter, softened
chardonnay-chocolate sauce (see
 recipe below)

Preheat oven to 375°. Carefully wash the outside of the pheasant and pat it dry.
Wipe the cavity with a clean damp cloth.

Combine the salt, pepper and thyme. Paint the inside of the bird with some of the
softened butter and sprinkle with some of the seasonings. Tie the legs together. Rub
the outside of the bird with the rest of the salt mixture. Either put the bird in a deep
roasting pan with a cover, or put into a roasting pan and cover securely with
aluminum foil. Put the covered pan in the oven and roast for 15 minutes before
reducing the heat to 350°. Cook for 1 hour 15 minutes. Test for doneness by
pressing your fingers against the flesh. If it feels springy, it is done. If the bird is not
cooked, the flesh will feel firm and tight. If not yet done, return to the oven and test
again after 12-15 minutes.

When the pheasant is done, let it rest uncovered for at least 5 minutes before
carving. Meanwhile prepare sauce.

Chardonnay-Chocolate Sauce:

2 tablespoons butter
½ cup finely chopped onions
2 medium garlic cloves, peeled and
 minced
1 tablespoon flour

¼ cup Northwest chardonnay
1 cup chicken stock, preferably freshly made
salt, pepper
2 teaspoons finely grated unsweetened
 baking chocolate

Melt butter in a sauté pan and when foaming stops, drop in the onions. Cook
until soft but not brown. Stir in minced garlic and toss for 1 minute. Then stir in
flour. Pour in the wine and stock and cook, stirring constantly until the sauce comes
to a boil and thickens slightly. Season to taste with salt and pepper. Add the
chocolate and stir constantly until chocolate has been incorporated. Taste and correct
seasoning.

Serves 4.

*A small, quietly elegant restaurant in the heart of downtown Spokane, Moreland's
specializes in fresh country cuisine and Northwest specialties with a French touch. Chef-
owner Billie Moreland has won many well-deserved plaudits since the restaurant opened
in 1972.*

CREDIT CARDS: V, MC, AE; SMOKING/NON-SMOKING; FULL BAR; RESERVATIONS RECOMMENDED
FOR DINNER

North 216 Howard Street, Skywalk Level • (509) 747-9830

THOMPSON'S
POINT OF VIEW

CANDIED YAMS

8 medium sized yams
⅓ cup packed brown sugar
1 cup white sugar
½ cup butter or margarine, melted
1 teaspoon cinnamon
½ teaspoon nutmeg
⅛ teaspoon cloves

Thoroughly wash and cook yams, whole, in water until just tender. Drain, reserving 1 cup liquid. Peel and cut yams into pieces approximately 2 inches long. Place in casserole dish. Combine the reserved liquid with the remaining ingredients. Pour over yams and bake, uncovered, at 400° for 30 minutes, basting 3-4 times.

Serves 6-8.

Thompson's Point of View was established in 1986. It features spicy and tantalizing Creole style cuisine together with the nostalgic goodness of "soul food" cooked to perfection. Owner Carl Thompson has assembled a staff dedicated to making one's visit an experience one will remember with pleasure and rush to repeat. House specialties include shrimp and crab gumbo and Creole Skillet Supreme.

CREDIT CARDS: V, MC; WHEELCHAIR ACCESS; FULL BAR; RESERVATIONS ACCEPTED
2308 East Union Street • (206) 329-2512

TESTA ROSSA

PESTO, PINENUTS, SUNDRIED TOMATOES STUFFED PIZZA

pizza sauce (see recipe below)
pesto (see recipe below)
1½ lbs. pizza dough (follow any basic recipe based on about 4 cups flour)
4 cups shredded Mozzarella cheese

¼ cup toasted pinenuts
¼ cup grated Parmesan cheese
10 sundried tomatoes, sliced finely
  (San Remo Pumate)

Prepare pizza sauce and pesto as directed. Prepare dough and let rise. Preheat oven to 475°.

Coat a 12-inch deep-dish pizza pan* generously with olive oil. Roll out two-thirds of dough to a 14-inch circle. Line pan so dough covers bottom and sides of pan and hangs over edge at least ¼ inch. Press dough to sides of pan so there are no air bubbles.

Paint a generous amount of pesto, about 1 cup, on bottom and sides of dough. Top with Mozzarella. Sprinkle with pinenuts. Roll out reserved portion of dough to a 12-inch circle. Place on top of cheese. Press the layers of dough together with fingertips. To create a seal, use a rolling pin and roll vigorously over the pan. Remove excess dough. Cut four 1-inch slits on top of dough.

Ladle 1½ cups pizza sauce on top of dough. Sprinkle with Parmesan. Bake for 25 minutes or until crust is golden brown. Remove pizza from pan and slice into 8 pieces. Top with sundried tomatoes.

* If not available, use two 8-inch cake pans. In this case, use half of the ingredients for each pan; also roll bottom layer of dough to a 10-inch circle and the top layer to an 8-inch one.

Pizza Sauce:

Sauté 5 cloves minced garlic in ¼ cup extra virgin olive oil for 1 minute. Add 1 tablespoon dried basil, 1½ teaspoons dried oregano and ¼ teaspoon crushed red chili peppers. Cook 30 seconds. Remove from heat. Add 1 (28 oz.) can Italian plum tomatoes, crushed, and ½ tablespoon brown sugar. Reserve 1½ cups for pizza; freeze remainder for another time.

Pesto:

Process 2 cups packed, fresh basil leaves, 6 cloves chopped garlic, ½ cup sweet butter, ½ cup toasted pinenuts, and ½ cup toasted walnuts in a food processor fitted with a steel blade. Add ½ cup extra virgin olive oil in a slow stream while machine is running. Remove mixture from bowl. Stir in Parmesan and salt and pepper to taste. Reserve approximately 1 cup for pizza; freeze remainder for another time.

4-5 servings.

Testa Rossa, "Redhead" in Italian, is an apt description of owner Andrea Williams who started Seattle's first and best Chicago-style stuffed pizza restaurant. Testa Rossa offers gourmet pizza in a romantic setting, using fresh ingredients from pesto and Italian fennel sausage to sun-dried tomatoes and roasted eggplant . But no pineapple. Unique appetizers, pasta dishes and desserts, accompanied with wine or beer of the same high quality, add to the allure of this Capitol Hill restaurant.

CREDIT CARDS: V, MC, AE; NON-SMOKING ONLY; BEER/WINE; RESERVATIONS AVAILABLE FOR PARTIES OF FIVE OR MORE

210 Broadway East • (206) 328-0878

PAUL'S PLACE

SEATTLE

CHICKEN BREAST WITH TARRAGON SAUCE

Tarragon Sauce:

4 tablespoons minced shallots
2 tablespoons butter
2 cups good chicken stock
2 cups heavy cream
2 tablespoons minced fresh tarragon

1 tablespoon minced fresh thyme
1 tablespoon minced parsley
1 tablespoon minced celery leaves
salt, pepper

Sweat shallots in butter. Add liquids and reduce to one cup. Add seasonings and simmer for 1 minute. Adjust with salt and pepper.

Chicken Preparation:

4 3 lb. chickens
12 stalks of chives
12 stalks of (5-inch ¼x¼)of celery
12 stalks of (5-inch ¼x¼)of carrots

½ cup brandy
4 stuffed tomatoes*
4 servings of buttered spinach

Bone out chicken breast with the whole skin left on (including the skin covering the leg meat). This is done by slitting the back of the chicken, scraping the meat off the bones, leaving it still attached to the skin. The leg and thigh are pulled out and used for another dish. The wing is cut off leaving as much skin as possible. Wishbone is then removed.

Place vegetables in middle of breast (3 stalks of each vegetable per breast). Add salt and pepper to taste. Roll meat over the vegetables and finish with skin wrapped around the stuffed breast. Tie chicken breast. Bake in 450° oven for 15 to 20 minutes. Do not overcook. Drain fat. Pour in brandy and flame. Add drippings to sauce and mix.

To Plate:

Remove string. Cut chicken into 3 pieces on the bias. Sauce plate. Place buttered spinach in middle and nest stuffed tomatoes on the spinach. Place chicken around the tomatoes.

* Use a ratatouille mixture for filling the tomatoes; or use halved tomatoes topped with a butter-Parmesan mixture and broiled.

Owner-chef Paul Lee, who trained at the Culinary Institute of America, brings his culinary skill and artistry to a devoted audience by adapting fresh seasonal Northwest ingredients in an intriguingly creative way. Paul's Place fabulous brunches are very popular, but breakfast, lunch, dinner, or brunch in this cozy, intimate converted house is a delightful experience.

CREDIT CARDS: V, MC, AE; SMOKING/NON-SMOKING SECTIONS; FULL BAR; RESERVATIONS REQUESTED

4741 Twelfth Avenue Northeast • (206) 523-9812

SURROGATE HOSTESS

SCONES WITH CURRANTS

3¼ cups flour
1½ teaspoons soda
¾ teaspoon salt
1½ teaspoons cream of tartar
1¼ to 1½ cups buttermilk
¾ cup currants
8 tablespoons (4 oz.) cold butter, cut into pieces

Preheat oven to 450°. In a mixing bowl or an electric mixer, combine the flour, soda, salt and cream of tartar. Add the butter and mix, until the mixture resembles coarse meal. Stir in the currants. Gradually add enough buttermilk, until the mixture is moist and soft, but not sticky. Do not overmix. Turn the dough out onto a floured surface and divide equally into three parts. Shape each piece into a ball and roll each ball into a flat round about ⅝ inch thick. Cut each round equally into four. Transfer the scones to a greased baking sheet, spacing one inch apart and bake at 450° for 12 to 15 minutes, until golden brown. Serve warm with butter and raspberry jam.

Whole wheat scones: substitute half whole wheat flour for the white flour.

Makes 1 dozen.

Surrogate Hostess, one of Capitol Hill's favorite cafeteria-style restaurants, serves breakfast, lunch and dinner seven days a week. Featuring American ethnic food, all the menu items served are created on the premises with rigorous emphasis on quality and freshness. In the midst of Sean Seedlock's popular gathering spot, the bakery produces a daily changing selection of mouthwatering temptations. Seedlock's scones are one of his customers' all-time favorites.

NO CREDIT CARDS; NON-SMOKING ONLY; BEER/WINE
746 Nineteenth Avenue East • (206) 324-1944

THE BLUE MOON
RESTAURANT
KENNEWICK

BEEF WASHINGTON DEMI-GLACE

1½ tablespoons unsalted butter
1½ tablespoons chopped shallots
2 oz. fresh mushrooms (about 10 medium)
2 tablespoons chardonnay
6 oz. beef tenderloin
1½ oz. liver pâté
3 tablespoons brandy
salt and pepper to taste
1 sheet 11" x 16" puff pastry dough, purchased from local bakery
egg wash (1 egg yolk mixed with 2 tablespoons water)
cooked baby carrots
parsley sprigs
demi-glace sauce (see recipe below)

Melt butter in sauté pan on medium heat. Meanwhile, process shallots and mushrooms in food processor with quick on-off bursts until finely chopped. Add to butter. Sauté, stirring constantly for 3 to 4 minutes. Add chardonnay and reduce until very little liquid remains in pan. Add tenderloin to processor and cut into ¼-inch pieces with on-off bursts. Remove to mixing bowl. Place pâté and brandy in processor and run until smooth. Add shallots, mushrooms, and pâté to tenderloin and mix thoroughly. Add salt and pepper to taste. Divide mixture into 6 equal-sized balls.

Cut dough in half and brush each half with egg wash. Place balls of meat mixture on one half of dough, spacing them evenly. Top with other half of dough. With a 3-inch crimp and cut tool, or a 3-inch glass, cut and seal each of the six appetizers. Remove excess dough and place each serving on a baking sheet. Brush tops with egg wash and cut a vent hole. Bake in a preheated oven at 375° for 15-20 minutes or until golden brown.

To serve, spoon 3 tablespoons demi-glace sauce onto each plate; top with pastry. Garnish with a baby carrot fan and sprigs of parsley.

Demi-Glace Sauce: Since demi-glace sauce is difficult and time consuming to make in the home kitchen, here is a simple and very successful version. Place 1 tablespoon unsalted butter in a small sauté pan and add 1 oz. of chopped shallots. Sauté until golden brown. Add ¾ cup water and ⅓ cup Merlot and bring to soft boil. Add 1½ oz. Knorr Swiss Demi-Glace Brown Sauce Mix (available at supermarkets and food specialty shops) and simmer 30 minutes. Remove from heat and strain through cheese cloth.

6 appetizer servings.

Once in a blue moon is how frequently a truly excellent restaurant comes into existence and thrives. This Blue Moon manages superb consistency in the quality of its cuisine, with the freshest, seasonal ingredients, innovative presentation, and casual elegance reflected in the strains of soft classical music and exquisite table settings in this seven-course oasis in the desert.

CREDIT CARDS: V, MC; NON-SMOKING ONLY; WINE ONLY; RESERVATIONS REQUIRED
21 West Canal Drive • (509) 582-6598

BANGKOK CAFE

SEATTLE

MEE KROB

4 oz. rice noodles
4 cups oil for deep frying
8 shrimp, peeled and deveined*
2 tablespoons diced bean cake (firm)
2 tablespoons tamarind juice
1 tablespoon tomato sauce
8 tablespoons sugar
1 tablespoon vinegar
1 teaspoon yellow bean sauce
1 egg (pan-fried, then sliced)
2 tablespoons pickled garlic slices
1 cup bean sprouts
1 tablespoon Chinese parsley
1 teaspoon diced red pepper
1 tablespoon chopped chives or green onion

Deep-fry noodles in hot oil until light brown. Set aside. Heat 2 tablespoons of remaining oil. Add shrimp and bean cake. Stir-fry until shrimp is cooked. Remove from heat.

In a large, deep saucepan, combine tamarind juice, tomato sauce, sugar, vinegar and yellow bean sauce. Bring to boil over medium heat. Stir constantly until syrup is formed. Add fried noodles; toss lightly until well-coated. Arrange on serving plate. Top with cooked shrimp and bean cake. Garnish with sliced fried egg, pickled garlic, bean sprouts, Chinese parsley, red pepper and chives or green onion. Then serve.

* Sliced beef, pork, or chicken can be used in place of shrimp.

4 servings (as part of a Thai meal).

The sister chefs, Gloy and Ooy, brought their home cooking from Thailand to Seattle in 1984. Fresh herbs and spices are prepared to perfection daily without using M.S.G. They specialize in vegetarian dishes and a variety of curries, while their full menu includes over 100 items. The lunch special changes daily.

CREDIT CARDS: V, MC, AE; SMOKING/NON-SMOKING SECTIONS
345 15th Avenue E • (206) 324-9443 • 4730 University Way NE • (206) 523-3220

R & L HOME OF
GOOD BARBEQUE
SEATTLE

PEACH COBBLER

Filling:

4 cups sliced fresh peaches or 2 (29 oz.) cans sliced peaches, drained
1½ cups sugar (1 cup if using canned peaches)
3 tablespoons flour
pinch salt (optional)
¼ teaspoon nutmeg
2½ tablespoons butter

Crust:

1 cup flour
¼ cup shortening
2 tablespoons water
¼ teaspoon salt

Preheat oven to 400°. To prepare filling, place peaches in a 2-quart casserole or baking dish. If peaches are fresh, heat until peaches start to simmer. Mix together sugar, flour, salt and nutmeg. Sprinkle over peaches; dot with butter.

To prepare crust, place flour in a bowl. Add shortening and salt. With fingertips, work in the shortening until mixture resembles coarse oatmeal. Mix in water. Roll out pastry on a floured board to ⅛ inch thick. Cut into strips; place strips horizontally and diagonally over the peaches. Bake for 45 minutes or until browned. Serve warm.

6-8 servings.

R & L Home of Good BBQ, Seattle's oldest BBQ restaurant, was established in 1952. The restaurant was passed on by the Rev. Collins and his wife Louise to their daughter Mary Davis who, with her daughters Barbara and Cheryl, and their cousin, Square Collins, the main cook, now own and run this unrivaled BBQ establishment. The menu includes ribs, beef brisket, chicken , Louisiana housemade beef hot links, baked beans, or potato salad—topped off with Mary Davis' luscious sweet potato pie or peach cobbler.

NO CREDIT CARDS; WHEELCHAIR ACCESS; SMOKING/NON-SMOKING; BEER/WINE;
NO RESERVATIONS

1816 East Yesler Way • (206) 322-0271

URUAPAN
MEXICAN RESTAURANT

COCHINITA PIBIL

2 lb. pork butt (pork shoulder)
1½ teaspoons salt
½ teaspoon pepper
½ teaspoon granulated garlic
½ small yellow onion, diced
2 cups water
2 large red skinned potatoes, boiled, peeled and cut in eighths (lengthwise)

Preheat oven to 400°. Slice pork ½ inch thick, in slices suitable for serving. Place slices in 13- by 9-inch baking pan. Add salt, pepper, garlic, onion and water. Bake covered for 30-40 minutes. While pork is cooking, boil potatoes and prepare Achiote sauce.

Remove pan with pork from oven; place potatoes on top of meat. Pour Achiote Sauce (see recipe below) over pork and potatoes. Bake 15 minutes at 350° (uncovered). Ready to serve.

Achiote Sauce:

⅓ bar Achiote (made from the red seeds of the Annato tree)
1 tablespoon cayenne
3 cups tomato juice
2 tablespoons red wine vinegar
juice from 1 medium orange
¼ teaspoon salt (optional)

In a blender, blend the Achiote, cayenne and tomato juice for a minute. Pour into a bowl and add vinegar and orange juice. Stir, mixing well. Add salt, if desired.

Note: More cayenne may be added if hotter taste is desired. Achiote bars are available at supermarkets in the Seattle area and also in Mexican food stores.

4-6 servings.

Suggested wine: Pink Chablis

Uruapan, "Sun of Eternal Spring," is in the state of Michoacan, Mexico. Owner-chef Guadalupe Ortiz is from there and has studied cooking there as well as in Mexico City and Oaxaca. Those who have visited Uruapan consider it their great fortune that she brought Uruapan-style cooking to Seattle. It is an exciting combination of French, Spanish, and Mexican-Indian cooking which keeps its guests coming back here—or to Lupe's other restaurant at 3508 Fremont Place North.

CREDIT CARDS: V, MC; BEER/WINE; NO RESERVATIONS
900 North One Hundred and Sixtieth • (206) 362-8725

WANZA
ETHIOPIAN CUISINE   SEATTLE

YE'ASSA IMMIS

4 medium white fish fillets, ½ inch thick (1½-2 lbs.)
2-4 tablespoons red pepper (berbere)* or red pepper paste (awaze)*
⅓ cup oil
½ cup white or red wine
¼ teaspoon black pepper
salt
2 small green peppers, finely chopped
1 medium onion, finely chopped

Cut fish into ½-inch pieces. Combine red pepper, oil, wine, pepper and salt to taste. Add fish, along with peppers and onions. Sauté over medium heat for 5-10 minutes or until fish is done. Serve with injera* or bread.

* available at the Wanza Restaurant

Note: for authentic Ethiopian spiciness, substitute 2 finely chopped, fresh jalepēno peppers for the green pepper.

4-6 servings.

Owner Ms. Alemayehv and her daughter created this cozy little restaurant in the University District so their guests could enjoy the communal experience of dining in the Ethiopian way. One may listen to the rhythm of a different land while sipping an imported wine or beer. They can savor exquisitely prepared chicken, lamb, beef or vegetarian dishes whose subtle spices will linger in the mind long after fading from the mouth. Wanza is an experience to remember.

CREDIT CARDS: V, MC; WHEELCHAIR ACCESS; BEER/WINE

6409 Roosevelt Way Northeast • (206) 525-3950

KARAM'S

LABAN AND LABNEN

Part of preparing laban (yogurt) and turning it into labnen (cream cheese) is easy and well worth learning, but the right temperature and environmental conditions are essential for success.

1 qt. fresh goat's milk
2 tablespoons commercial plain goat or cow's milk yogurt or starter from previous batch
1 heavy wool blanket or jacket

Heat (do not boil) milk in a pot until a froth arises. Remove from heat. Cool to the point where you can hold your little finger in the milk for a count of ten before the sting of the heat is felt. The yogurt could fail if it is any hotter or cooler than this. Combine 2 tablespoons commercial yogurt with ½ cup of the warm milk. Add to rest of milk, mixing well. Cover with lid and wrap entire pot with heavy wool blanket. Leave undisturbed in warm (not hot), draft-free place overnight or no longer than 10 hours; otherwise yogurt will taste too sour. Place in refrigerator until cold—approximately 4 to 6 hours.

Labnen:

refrigerated laban
½ teaspoon salt
1 tightly woven cheese cloth bag or white cotton pillow case (boil to sterilize)
3 cloves garlic
½ teaspoon dried mint
⅛ teaspoon salt

⅛ teaspoon pepper
zatar - a combination of sesame seeds, finely ground oregano, marjoram, salt and sumac*
sumac - dried crushed berries of a sumac tree, lemony in flavor*
pure virgin olive oil*

Add ½ teaspoon salt and ¼ cup water to laban. Mix well. Pour laban into cheese cloth bag and hang over a bowl to drip for 1 to 2 days. The whey will drain away, leaving a very light, soft, creamy white cheese. Scoop cheese from bag into a bowl. Blend in puréed mixture of three cloves garlic, ½ teaspoon dried mint, ⅛ teaspoon salt and ⅛ teaspoon pepper. Swirl a portion onto a plate with the back of a soup spoon. Sprinkle with the zatar and sumac. Then sprinkle with pure virgin olive oil. Top with several calamata olives. Tear off a piece of pita bread and enjoy!

   * can be purchased at import food stores

Karam's glows with the pride and passion of Julie and Anis Karam who oversee every delicious detail in this delightful restaurant. The ideas and recipes are perfected with love and attention to quality and freshness. Besides traditional Lebanese chicken, lamb, fish, falafil and hummus, the Karams are proud of their exciting selection of wines from Lebanon, Morocco and Algeria.

CREDIT CARDS: V, MC; CHECKS ACCEPTED; SMOKING/NON-SMOKING; BEER/WINE; RESERVATIONS PREFERRED

340 Fifteenth Avenue East • (206) 324-2370

BRAVO

BELLEVUE

MELANZANE TIMBALE

Eggplant:

1 medium eggplant
1 teaspoon salt
5 oz. (10 tablespoons) olive oil

Filling:

4 oz. goat cheese
16 oz. ricotta cheese
2 oz. Parmesan cheese
1 egg yolk
pinch marjoram
½ teaspoon white pepper

Tomato Sauce:

2 tablespoons olive oil
¼ white onion, chopped
½ carrot, chopped
½ celery stalk, chopped
2 (28 oz.) cans Italian pear tomatoes in juice
3 large fresh basil leaves
½ teaspoon salt
¼ teaspoon fresh ground pepper

Italian parsley for garnish

To prepare eggplant, trim off ends but leave skin on. Slice eggplant lengthwise into ¼-inch thick slices. Place slices on a large baking sheet. Lightly salt and let stand about 1 hour. Pat slices dry with paper towels. Heat oil (not smoking) in a large skillet. Fry eggplant slices, a few at a time, until soft but not mushy. Drain on paper towels, patting dry to remove excess oil. Set aside to cool.

To prepare filling, place all ingredients in a food processor; blend until smooth. Set aside.

To prepare tomato sauce, heat oil in a medium skillet. Add onion, carrot and celery. Sauté until soft. Add tomatoes and basil. Cook for 1 hour. Put mixture through a food mill, or blend in a food processor, and then strain. Return to skillet. Cook on medium heat, stirring constantly. When sauce has reduced to one-third, adjust with salt and pepper and set aside.

To prepare timbales, lightly oil six 6 oz. soufflé cups. Arrange just enough eggplant slices in an overlapping pattern to cover entire bottom and sides of cup, leaving enough excess to cover and seal in filling. Spoon cheese mixture into cups, mounding ¼ inch over top. Fold eggplant over cheese mixture to seal. Refrigerate 1 hour to set. Unmold timbales carefully. Place on lightly oiled baking pan. Bake in a preheated 400° oven for 10-12 minutes.

To serve, place tomato sauce on bottom of each plate. Remove timbales from baking pan with a spatula; place on top of sauce. Garnish with parsley. Serve hot.

6 appetizer servings.

Bravo serves exceptional Italian food with the ambience of an Italian villa. An open kitchen fulfills the menu's promise of excellence, from traditional Italian dishes to novel adaptations using fresh seafood, aged beef, veal and fresh pasta, all prepared by chef Walter Pisano. A wood-fired oven and gourmet pizzas lend just the right touch of informality.

CREDIT CARDS: V, MC, AE; WHEELCHAIR ACCESS; SMOKING/NON-SMOKING SECTIONS; FULL BAR; RESERVATIONS REQUIRED

10733 Northup Way • (206) 827-8585

AYUTTHAYA
THAI RESTAURANT

LARB NEAU

½ lb. very lean ground beef
1-2 tablespoons lime juice
2 tablespoons fish sauce
1 teaspoon chili powder
1 teaspoon rice powder*
2 green onions, sliced
¼ cup chopped red onion
lettuce leaves
sprigs of mint and cilantro
diagonally sliced cucumbers

In a saucepan, cook ground beef over medium heat for about 10 minutes. Do not overcook! Place in a mixing bowl. Add lime juice, fish sauce, chili powder, rice powder, green onions and red onions. Mix together. Spoon over a bed of lettuce leaves. Garnish with mint, cilantro and cucumber slices. To eat, scoop up meat mixture with lettuce leaves.

* To prepare rice powder, wash 1 tablespoon rice; drain and brown in a pan (without oil) over low heat. Pound or grind to a fine powder.

2 appetizer servings.

Ayutthaya and its sister restaurant, the Thai Restaurant (see p. 189), are two of the very best of all the Thai restaurants which have opened recently in response to the tremendous popularity of Thai food. Ayutthaya and Thai are owned and operated by the Fuangaromya family whose restaurants are the best proof of their claim to be in business more for the joy of sharing their food and culture than for making money. The mother, Sasom Fuangaromya, is the chef and she loves preparing authentic Thai food for their appreciative customers.

CREDIT CARDS: V, MC, AE; WHEELCHAIR ACCESS; NON-SMOKING SECTION; BEER/WINE; RESERVATIONS ACCEPTED

727 East Pike Street • (206) 324-8833

PAPARAZZI   SEATTLE

PENNE MEDITERRANEAN

2 lb. whole, white fish, such as snapper, cod, or yellowtail (also salmon or tuna)
2 quarts water
½ bunch parsley
1 lemon, cut in quarters
1 stalk celery, top included
3 medium onions
¼ cup olive oil
2 green peppers, cut in 1-inch cubes
1 red pepper, cut in 1-inch cubes
¼ teaspoon crushed red chile peppers
6 bay leaves
1 tablespoon dried sweet basil
1 tablespoon Greek oregano
3 cloves garlic, finely chopped

2 oz. capers
½ cup Greek olives, pitted
1 (12 oz.) can Italian tomatoes in heavy purée or 1½ cups crushed Italian tomatoes in purée
2 cups white wine
1 lb. Manilla steamer clams
1 lb. Penn Cove mussels
½ lb. singing (pink) scallops
½ lb. calamari, cleaned and cut into wide rings
1 lb. Black Tiger prawns (16 per lb.), peeled and deveined
12 oz. Florida bay scallops (large)
lemon wedges, watercress, parsley for garnish

Start by making a Puttanesca sauce. Fillet fish, retaining all scraps. Set filleted portion aside. Place fish scraps, excluding any internal organs, in a medium-sized sauce pan. Cover with water. Add parsley and lemon and place over medium-high heat. Place top and butt portion of celery stock in a sauté pan, heated with 2 tablespoons olive oil. Cut one onion into sixths, skin and all, and add to celery. Sauté vegetables until al dente. Add to fish stock. Lower heat and simmer until reduced by half.

While stock is reducing, cut remaining piece of celery and the two onions into 1-inch cubes. In a medium saucepan, sauté celery, onion and sweet pepper chunks in 2 tablespoons olive oil until tender. Add chiles, bay leaves, basil, oregano, garlic, capers and olives. Cook over medium heat for about 10 minutes, stirring occasionally.

Strain fish stock through an extra fine sieve or cheesecloth. Add to sautéed vegetables. Stir in tomatoes. Simmer until Puttanesca becomes thick, about an hour.

In a large sauté pan (large enough to hold all ingredients), place the Puttanesca sauce (about 4 cups), white wine, clams, mussels and singing scallops. Cover and cook on medium-high until shellfish open, about 8 minutes. Cube filleted fish into 1-inch pieces. Lower heat to medium-low and add fish, calamari, prawns and scallops. Cover and simmer about 12 minutes or until all seafood is done.

Arrange clams and mussels around edge of a large serving platter. Remove pink scallops and prawns from sauce and set aside. Using a slotted spoon, remove remaining seafood and vegetables and spoon into the middle of the platter. Return sauce to high heat, and reduce to a thick, rich sauce. Arrange prawns and scallops decoratively over top of dish. Pour sauce over all. Garnish with lemon wedges, watercress and parsley.

4-6 servings.

Paparazzi is a family operated restaurant offering exceptional Italian cuisine in an atmosphere of old-world elegance and quiet conversation. The narrow, sophisticated dining room, adorned with exciting contemporary art, renews the spirit, nourishes the soul and stimulates the palate. Not to be missed are the weekend breakfasts and lunches, both served all day.

CREDIT CARDS: V, MC, AE; CHECKS ACCEPTED; WHEELCHAIR ACCESS; SMOKING/NON-SMOKING SECTIONS; BEER/WINE; RESERVATIONS RECOMMENDED; FREE PARKING

2202 North Forty-fifth Street • (206) 547-7772

THE PALM COURT   SEATTLE
ROAST LOIN OF VEAL STUFFED WITH LOBSTER

4 whole lobster tails (see preparation
  below)
2 lbs. boned loin of veal
⅔ cup veal stock

¼ cup sherry vinegar
¼ cup Armagnac
4 tablespoons cold butter
salt and freshly ground pepper

Prepare lobster tails as directed.

With a thin-pointed knife blade, make an incision the length of the loin and stuff with the lobster tails. Preheat the oven to 350°. Place the loin in the oven and cook to an internal temperature of 165°. Remove the meat; let the meat rest while you finish the sauce. Pour out all the grease from the pan. Add veal stock to the pan. Over medium heat, scrape all the browned particles into the stock. Then rapidly reduce the liquid by one-half; add vinegar and Armagnac and reduce by half again or until you have only ½ cup liquid left. Turn off heat and whisk in the cold butter, tablespoon by tablespoon. Season with salt and freshly ground pepper. Carve the meat into ¼-inch slices. Pour the sauce on each of 4 warmed dinner plates. Place 4 pieces of stuffed veal loin on each plate. Serve additional vegetable garnishes around the sauce.

Sautéed Washington pears with raspberry sauce would be an excellent dessert or asparagus spears in a puff pastry pillow with hollandaise sauce can precede this simple roast.

Preparation of Lobster Tails:

¾ cup sliced carrots
½ cup sliced onions
4 shallots, peeled and sliced
1 garlic clove, peeled and sliced
sprig of thyme
½ bay leaf

parsley sprig
salt, white peppers
1½ cups white wine
2 cups water
4 1¼ lb. live lobsters

To make the court-bouillon, place carrots, onions, shallots and garlic in a large pot. Boil them with thyme, bay leaf, washed parsley, salt and pepper in the white wine and water for five minutes.

Add a little more water if necessary and bring back to a rolling boil. Add lobsters headfirst one after another. Cover the pot and simmer for 15 minutes. Drain the lobster and shell the tail whole.

4 servings.

The Palm Court is always in the forefront of eating trends thanks to chef Graeme Watson. The cuisine is continental with strong Northwest infusions. The daily fresh sheet might include wild boar with Calvados cream sauce. The setting in the Westin Hotel is magnificent with two distinct day and night personalities. The service is meticulous and the dining is elegant, yet simple.

CREDIT CARDS: V, MC, AE, DC; WHEELCHAIR ACCESS; RESERVATIONS RECOMMENDED
The Westin Hotel 1900 Fifth Avenue • (206) 728-1000

WANG'S GARDEN
ROAST PEKING DUCK

BELLEVUE

1 duck (specially fed, fat, about 5 lbs.)
3 tablespoons honey (or molasses)
2 tablespoons wine
1 tablespoon vinegar
1 cup hot water
3 tablespoons soy bean paste (or Hoisin sauce)
1 tablespoon sesame oil
2 tablespoons sugar
½ cup water
10-12 green onions (white part only)
10-12 Mandarin pancakes or flour tortillas

Clean outside of duck and cut off neck and feet. Rinse inside until water comes clean. Pat dry.

Combine honey, wine, vinegar and hot water. Bring to boil. In a large bowl, baste duck thoroughly with hot syrup mixture, until skin is tight. Use two small sticks to brace the wings away from the body. Tie a string around the neck and hang in a drafty place. Let wind dry for about 6-8 hours or overnight.

To cook, roast in a rotisserie for about 30-40 minutes. Duck may also be baked in an oven. Place on a small rack in a baking pan and bake at 325° for 20 minutes. Turn and bake 20 minutes longer or until skin is golden brown and crisp.

Slice all of the duck skin into thin pieces; then slice meat. Combine soy bean paste or Hoisin sauce, sesame oil, sugar and water. Bring to a boil and cook 30 seconds. Serve duck with bean paste sauce, tortillas or pancakes and green onions.

To eat, spoon some sauce onto a pancake; top with a green onion; add 1-2 pieces of crisp duck and roll up.

10-12 servings.

Wang's Garden is the Nothwest's only Chinese garden and restaurant serving Imperial cuisine. Guests can walk through the beautiful garden and then experience a meal fit for an emperor, prepared by master chef and owner Mr. C. C. Wang. Eating at Wang's Garden is a real adventure in gourmet Chinese cuisine.

CREDIT CARDS: V, MC, AE, DC; WHEELCHAIR ACCESS; SMOKING/NON-SMOKING SECTIONS; FULL BAR; RESERVATIONS REQUESTED

1644 One Hundred and Fortieth Northeast • (206) 641-6011

THAI RESTAURANT SEATTLE

LOBSTER-LAD-PRIG

one 3 lb. live lobster
2 tablespoons oil
1 oz. canned straw mushrooms, chopped
2 cloves garlic, chopped
2 tablespoons brown sugar
1-5 red chile peppers, chopped (fresh or dried)
1 tablespoon fish sauce
5 fresh or dried Kaffir lime leaves, chopped (soak dried leaves to soften)*
1 tablespoon cornstarch
½ cup cold water
10 basil leaves, chopped
½ red and green chile pepper, sliced (fresh or dried)

Cut lobster, shell and all, into 8 or 9 pieces (see note below). Rinse well. Crack claws.

Heat oil in a large pan. Add mushrooms and garlic and cook over medium heat until golden brown. Add brown sugar, chopped chile peppers, fish sauce and lime leaves. Mix well.

Dissolve cornstarch in water and add to sauce. Stir well. Stir in lobster and reduce heat. Add basil and simmer until lobster is cooked. Place on large platter. Garnish with sliced green and red chile peppers.

Note: Cut off head, first. Then cut off legs and claws, discarding small hairy legs. Cut body and head in half lengthwise. Remove vein, stomach, eyes, and antennae and discard. Cut the parts into pieces.

* available at Oriental markets

4-6 servings.

The Fuangaromya family who own and run the Thai Restaurant and Ayutthaya (see page 100) say the secret to Thai cooking is the mixture of fresh ingredients and seasonings, which may seem complex but are mostly available at any good grocery: garlic, shallots, basil, coriander and chile pepper. It's the right blend and balance that make the difference, and, of course, the fact that all their curries and seasonings are from Thailand. The Fuangaromyas' restaurants are also exceptional because they insist on making every dish perfect rather than accommodating as many customers as possible.

CREDIT CARDS: V, MC, AE; WHEELCHAIR ACCESS; SMOKING/NON-SMOKING SECTIONS; FULL BAR
101 John Street • (206) 285-9000

PHILADELPHIA
FEVRE STEAK AND HOAGIE SHOP SEATTLE

MUSHROOM PEPPER CHEESESTEAK

1 lb. rib eye steak meat or eye roast
vegetable oil
3 oz. finely chopped onions (about ⅔ cup)
½ cup sliced mushrooms
½ cup sliced pickled cherry peppers (hot or sweet)
8 slices white American cheese (½-1 oz. each)
four 6-inch Italian rolls
salt and pepper
suggested condiments — ketchup, mustard or steak sauce

Partially freeze meat and slice or chip very thinly against the grain. Set grill or heat frying pan at medium heat. Place a little oil on frying surface and brown onion. Add steak and, while frying, gently pull apart to produce a shredded texture. If steak becomes too dry, add more oil. Add mushrooms and peppers and continue to fry until peppers soften slightly. Place all cheese on the steak and allow to melt. Scoop mixture into Italian rolls. Season to taste with salt and pepper. Add condiments as desired.

Serves 4.

"Philadelphia Fevre is the 'real thing' in authentic Philadelphia sandwiches and hoagies—without the 3,000 mile trip," laughs Renee Le Fevre. Patrons can see the sights of Philly, browse through the Philadelphia magazine or the Philadelphia Daily News while their cheesesteak sizzles. Nowhere else in the Pacific Northwest can one experience the gourmet delight of an imported Philadelphia Tastycake. The Philadelphia Fevre is the friendly favorite in the Madison Valley.

CREDIT CARDS: V, MC, AE, DISC; WHEELCHAIR ACCESS; BEER; NO RESERVATIONS
2332 East Madison Street • (206) 323-1000

HUNAN HARBOR

SEATTLE

GENERAL TSO'S CHICKEN

12 oz. boneless drumstick meat, cut in 2-inch pieces (about 6 medium drumsticks, each cut into about 4 pieces)
½ egg white
½ teaspoon salt
1 teaspoon cornstarch
½ teaspoon white pepper
salad oil
7-8 small, dry hot Japanese peppers
1 teaspoon minced garlic
½ teaspoon grated ginger
2 tablespoons chopped green onion
1 tablespoon sugar
2 tablespoons soy sauce
½ tablespoon vinegar
½ tablespoon sesame oil

Marinate drumstick meat in a mixture of egg white, salt, cornstarch, white pepper and 1 tablespoon salad oil for 2 hours.

Deep-fry chicken pieces in 1 quart salad oil for about 7-8 minutes, or until crispy and golden brown. Drain. In a clean wok, heat ¼ cup oil. "Burn" Japanese peppers by cooking them for a few seconds in hot oil. Then stir in remaining ingredients. Add chicken and stir-fry for about 1 minute.

4 servings (as part of a Chinese meal).

Located on Lake Union, Hunan Harbor is Seattle's only waterfront Chinese restaurant. Authentic Hunan, Szechwan and Mandarin cuisine at Angela Chen's picturesque place has earned her kudos. They offer view banquet seating for parties of up to 200 and, much to the locals' delight, free home or office delivery.

CREDIT CARDS: V, MC, AE; SMOKING/NON-SMOKING SECTIONS; FULL BAR; RESERVATIONS FOR FIVE OR MORE

2040 Westlake Avenue North • (206) 285-1242

PATIT CREEK RESTAURANT

DAYTON

LAMB CHOPS WITH ROASTED GARLIC CREAM SAUCE

1 head garlic
2 tablespoons olive oil
8 center-cut loin lamb chops, 1 inch thick
salt and freshly ground pepper
½ cup cognac
½ cup dry red wine
2 cups beef stock, preferably homemade, or canned beef consommé
1 cup whipping cream
4 tablespoons butter, at room temperature
sautéed whole garlic cloves (optional)*

Heat oven to 350°. Roast whole garlic, wrapped in foil, until soft, about 30-40 minutes. Remove from oven and cool. Reduce heat to 200°. Squeeze pulp from garlic cloves and mix with 1 tablespoon olive oil.

Season lamb chops with salt and pepper to taste. Heat remaining tablespoon of olive oil in heavy skillet over high heat. Add half of the lamb chops. Sauté until desired doneness is reached (about 4 minutes per side for medium rare). Place in warm oven. Repeat with remaining chops. Keep chops warm while preparing sauce.

Drain oil from skillet and add cognac, wine, beef stock and garlic purée. Boil until reduced by half. Add cream and continue to cook until thick. Remove pan from heat. Taste, and add salt and pepper if needed. Whisk in butter, 1 tablespoon at a time. Divide sauce among four plates. Place chops on sauce. If desired, garnish with sautéed garlic cloves.

* To prepare sautéed whole garlic cloves, boil peeled garlic cloves in water for 5 minutes. Sauté in olive oil over medium-low heat until nut brown. Drain on paper towel.

4 servings.

Nestled on the edge of the Blue Mountains in the small farming hamlet of Dayton, Bruce and Heather Hiebert have created an acclaimed French-influenced cuisine in a charming atmosphere reminiscent of a French country inn. At Patit Creek their full-service menu boasts only the freshest Northwest produce.

CREDIT CARDS: V, MC; WHEELCHAIR ACCESS; BEER/WINE; RESERVATIONS RECOMMENDED
725 East Dayton Avenue • (509) 382-2625

1 lb. lean, boneless pork loin
½ lb. pancetta (Italian bacon)
3-4 tablespoons finely minced garlic
2 tablespoons chopped Italian parsley
1 teaspoon black pepper
flour
¼ cup olive oil
1 teaspoon salt
1 cup water
1 cup Italian dry white wine
sautéed fresh vegetables

Slice pork thinly into 12 slices. Pound out thin. Grind pancetta and mix in garlic, parsley and pepper. Lay out pork slices and place approximately 2 tablespoons bacon mixture on narrow end of each slice. Roll up very tightly and tie off with thread. Flour each roll lightly. Heat oil in skillet over high heat. Add rolls and cook until lightly browned, about 5 minutes. Sprinkle with salt while browning. Add water and wine. Reduce heat to medium. Cook until sauce thickens, about 15 minutes. (Thicken with flour if necessary.)

To serve, place rolls on platter. Pour sauce over top. Garnish with sautéed vegetables.

Il Paesano has been a family affair since Gianfranco and Rhonda Bafaro opened its doors in 1985. With a southern Italian theme, the menu contains red sauce aplenty, fresh fish, and hand-tossed pizza to dream about. Checkered floor and tablecloths add to the cozy European atmosphere. The Bafaros recently opened another restaurant at 132 Lake Street South in Kirkland named Calabria, for the region in Italy from which they come.

CREDIT CARDS: V, MC; WHEELCHAIR ACCESS; BEER/WINE; NO RESERVATIONS

5628 University Way Northeast • (206) 526-0949

RAY'S BOATHOUSE SEATTLE

RED KING SALMON WITH BASIL BEURRE BLANC

6 oz. chardonnay
3 oz. white wine vinegar
3 oz. fish stock
4 oz. shallots
six 8 oz. red king salmon fillets
seasoned flour (salt and white pepper added)
4 oz. (½ cup) clarified butter
10 oz. (1¼ cup) butter
pinch white pepper
⅓ cup chopped fresh basil
juice of ¼ lemon

Reduce chardonnay, vinegar, fish stock and shallots in stainless or copper pan to just more than a glaze. Remove sauce from heat.

Lightly dredge salmon in seasoned flour and brown both sides in clarified butter. Place in 450° oven to finish.

Reheat sauce base to just below boil. Slowly swirl in small pieces of butter. Add white pepper, basil, and juice of ¼ lemon.

Remove fish from oven when done; nap with sauce and serve immediately.

6 servings.

Ray's Boathouse has a tradition of dealing directly with fishermen, growers, producers and harvesters to obtain only the freshest and most ideal products available. The very best of these products are chosen and prepared simply and with respect for their natural integrity. This simple presentation of excellent quality is carried forth in all aspects of the restaurant, including decor, service and a genuine caring for people.

CREDIT CARDS: V, MC, AE, DC; WHEELCHAIR ACCESS; SMOKING/NON-SMOKING SECTIONS; FULL BAR; RESERVATIONS RECOMMENDED

6049 Seaview Avenue Northwest • (206) 789-3770

THE ROADHOUSE COLVILLE
YELLOW SUMMER SQUASH CASSEROLE

8-10 yellow crookneck squash (the smaller the better), cut in 1-inch chunks
1 large onion, diced
salt to taste (about 1 teaspoon)
½ teaspoon pepper
¼ lb. (½ cup) butter, melted
3 eggs, well-beaten
1½ cups milk
8 oz. mild Cheddar cheese, grated
2 tablespoons flour
1 cup bread crumbs

Steam squash and onion in vegetable steamer until tender. Drain water completely. Mash with potato masher. Add salt and pepper. Stir in remaining ingredients except bread crumbs; mix well. Pour into a shallow 3-quart baking dish. Bake, uncovered, at 350° for about 1 hour. Top with bread crumbs 30 minutes before casserole is done.

8 servings.

The Roadhouse, a restored turn-of-the-century farmhouse overlooking the beautiful Colville Valley, is more than a restaurant—it is a philosophy. Sara Lee Pilley carries on the Southern styles of cooking and serving, including offering mint juleps with fresh mint, that "have so long nourished not only the body but the soul." Being a guest in this small family-owned restaurant is like "coming home to eat."

CREDIT CARDS: V, MC, AE, DC; WHEELCHAIR ACCESS; SMOKING/NON-SMOKING SECTIONS; FULL BAR; RESERVATIONS REQUIRED FOR DINNER

½ mile south of Colville on U.S. 395 • (509) 684-3021

MISTY'S
ABERDEEN
MISTY'S PASTA SALAD WITH CHICKEN BREAST PAUPIETTES

4 oz. prosciutto, cut into thin strips
1 cup broken pecans
¾ cup crumbled Roquefort
⅓ cup snipped parsley
⅓ cup olive oil
2 tablespoons fresh rosemary

½ teaspoon ground pepper
1 clove garlic, minced
8 oz. bow tie pasta, cooked and drained
freshly grated Parmesan cheese to taste
Misty's Chicken Paupiettes (see recipe
below)

Combine all ingredients except pasta, Parmesan cheese and chicken. Cover and marinate in refrigerator for 30 minutes. Add pasta and Parmesan cheese. Refrigerate until serving time. Remove rolled Misty's Chicken Paupiettes from plastic wrap. Slice diagonally and arrange on salad. (Add vegetable embellishment upon personal whim.)

Misty's Chicken Paupiettes:

2 tablespoons butter
2 bunches fresh spinach (about 2 lbs.)
   stemmed
2 tablespoons olive oil
6 oz. wild mushrooms (such as
   chanterelles, shitake or morels),
   trimmed and thinly sliced

3 cloves garlic, minced
salt and freshly ground pepper to taste
eight 5 oz. boned chicken breast halves,
   skinned
2 quarts chicken stock

Melt butter in heavy skillet over medium heat. Add spinach and sauté until wilted, but still bright green, about 2 minutes. Drain and cool slightly. Using hands, squeeze all excess moisture from spinach.

Heat olive oil in heavy skillet over medium heat. Add mushrooms and garlic and sauté until they begin to exude liquid, about 2 minutes. Season with salt and pepper.

Place chicken breast halves between sheets of waxed paper. Pound to ¼-inch thickness. Pat chicken dry. Season with salt and pepper. Set each breast on a 10-inch square of plastic wrap. Cover each with ⅛ of mushrooms, and then ⅛ of spinach. Roll chicken up into cylinders. Twist and tie ends of plastic wrap to seal completely. Bring chicken stock to boil. Reduce heat to simmer. Add chicken and poach 12 minutes. Remove from stock and keep warm.

8 servings.

Probably the best way to convey the essence of Misty's is to quote owner-chef Tracy P. Walthall directly: "Food isn't of a solitary nature. Food has never made sense to me without its surroundings—the eye, as well as the palate, has to be won. In choosing Misty's daily menu I'm always aware of color and texture. They can dazzle or they can dull. Entertaining is a lifelong love—the felicitous part of my life. I approach restaurant-life with integrity and passion so that other lovers of the Pacific Northwest can share in my personal culinary delights. Only an environment as generous as the Northwest could inspire both my own and my guests' loyalty and devotion to Misty's. My heartfelt motto is 'cooking is like love...it should be entered into with abandon...or not at all.'"

CREDIT CARDS: V, MC, AE; WHEELCHAIR ACCESS; BEER/WINE; RESERVATIONS ACCEPTED
116 West Heron Street • (206) 533-0956

AFGHAN HORSEMAN
SEATTLE

MANTU

1 lb. ground beef or lamb
2 teaspoons salt
1 lb. onions, finely chopped
1 green chile pepper
1-2 teaspoons ground black pepper
1-2 teaspoons ground cumin
1 teaspoon vegetable oil
1 teaspoon finely chopped fresh coriander
wonton wrappers
yogurt
sour cream
crushed fresh garlic

Combine beef, salt, onions, chile peppers, black pepper, cumin, oil and coriander. Mix well. Spoon a heaping tablespoon of meat mixture in center of each wonton wrapper. Moisten edges with milk. Then bring 2 opposite corners together in the center, pinching to seal. Repeat with remaining 2 sides, pinching edges to seal. Place on greased steaming rack or tray. Steam for 20-25 minutes.

Combine equal parts of sour cream and yogurt. Add garlic to taste. Serve as a sauce for hot mantu.

Makes 3 dozen.

Afghanistan is a country rich in traditions, social customs, and foods. Afghan Horseman owner Aziz Sadat proudly continues this tradition at his unique little restaurant in the University District and claims "Afghan food is as tasty as any in the world."

NO CREDIT CARDS; NON-SMOKING; PERSONAL CHECKS ACCEPTED

5517 University Way Northeast • (206) 525-0658

LINDAMAN'S

SPOKANE

GOLDEN CHOCOLATE TORTE

Chocolate Cake:

¼ cup cocoa powder
½ cup boiling water
¾ cup flour
1 cup sugar
¾ teaspoon baking soda
½ teaspoon salt
4 egg yolks
1 teaspoon vanilla
¼ cup oil
12 egg whites
¼ teaspoon cream of tartar

Dark Chocolate Frosting (see recipe on page 211)
White Chocolate Frosting (see recipe on page 211)
Candied violets

Meringue:

4 egg whites
1⅓ cups sugar
3 tablespoons cocoa powder
1 tablespoon white wine
vinegar
½ teaspoon vinegar

Filling:

8 oz. semi-sweet chocolate
3 tablespoons butter
2½ tablespoons coffee liqueur
2½ tablespoons Triple Sec
3 eggs, separated
1½ tablespoons light brown
sugar, firmly packed
1 tablespoon instant coffee
powder
1⅓ cup whipping cream
pinch cream of tartar and salt,
each
2 tablespoons powdered
sugar

To prepare meringue, preheat oven to 350°. Line 2 cookie sheets with parchment paper. Beat egg whites until thick and foamy, adding sugar, 1 tablespoon at a time. Beat until stiff peaks form. Gently fold in cocoa, vinegar and vanilla. Spoon onto parchment-lined pans shaping into two 9-inch circles (one on each pan). Bake for 30-35 minutes. Remove from paper; then cool.

To prepare chocolate cake, preheat oven to 350°. Paper, butter and flour a 9-inch springform pan. Mix cocoa with boiling water and set aside. Place flour, sugar, baking soda, salt, egg yolks, vanilla, oil and cocoa mixture in bowl and mix well. Beat egg whites with cream of tartar until stiff but not dry. Gently fold into cake batter. Pour into prepared pan and bake for about 45 minutes. Cool in pan.

To prepare filling, melt chocolate and butter in microwave or in a double boiler. Add liqueurs, egg yolks, brown sugar and coffee powder to chocolate mixture. Whip cream until stiff and gently fold into chocolate mixture. Beat egg whites with cream of tartar and salt until thick and foamy, adding powdered sugar 1 tablespoon at a time. Beat until stiff but not dry. Gently fold into chocolate mixture.

To assemble torte, slice cake in half, crosswise. Place bottom layer on plate; then alternate filling and meringues, ending with the remaining cake layer on top. Chill about 4 hours. Frost top and sides of torte with dark chocolate frosting, reserving some for decoration. Using a leaf pastry tip, pipe dark chocolate leaves around top edge of cake with reserved frosting. Then, with white chocolate frosting, pipe leaves in an interesting pattern next to dark ones. Place candied violets at base of some of the leaves. Chill until set, about 1 hour.   12 servings.

Lindaman's, situated in a single story brick building built in the 20's, is a beloved local institution. The food is served delicatessen style in the wonderful dining room (with its exposed brick walls, hardwood floors and lots of big windows) which seats about fifty. David and Marilee Lindaman offer a dozen hot casseroles, as well as many home-made desserts and salads, all of which change daily, resulting in a menu that has thousands of new items in the course of a year. This variety brings hundreds of customers in three to four times a week, creating quite a coffeehouse comraderie. There is also a large espresso bar and an excellent selection of fine wines.

CREDIT CARDS: V, MC; WHEELCHAIR ACCESS; NON-SMOKING ONLY; BEER/WINE

1235 South Grand Avenue • (509) 838-3000

brusseau's

CLASSIC RUSSIAN KULEBIAKA

Buttery Brioche:

½ lb. butter
½ cup honey
4 eggs
3 cakes (.6 oz.) fresh yeast
3 cups water
1 tablespoon salt
8-9 cups flour

Filling:

8 tablespoons unsalted butter
½ lb. fresh mushrooms, thinly sliced
3 tablespoons fresh, strained lemon
  juice
1½ teaspoons salt
freshly ground black pepper
3 cups finely chopped onions

Poached Salmon:

2 cups dry white wine
1 cup coarsely chopped onions
½ cup coarsely chopped celery
1 cup scraped coarsely chopped carrots
10 whole black peppercorns
1 tablespoon salt
2½ lb. fresh salmon fillet, in one piece

½ cup unconverted, long grain rice
1 cup chicken stock, fresh or canned
⅓ cup finely cut fresh dill leaves
3 hard-cooked eggs, finely chopped
1 large bunch spinach, stemmed, rinsed
  and dried
1 cup sour cream

To prepare brioche dough, blend butter and honey until smooth. Add remaining ingredients, adding only 6 cups of the flour. Mix well. Knead with a dough hook or food processor until dough pulls away from sides of bowl, adding remaining 2-3 cups flour, a little at a time. This takes about 15-20 minutes with dough hook. (If necessary, dough can be kneaded in a large bowl using a scraper or spatula.) Please note: This dough is very soft and smooth, appearing almost runny while mixing. Refrigerate dough in a covered bowl overnight.

To poach salmon, bring 3 quarts water to boil with ingredients, except salmon. Add salmon and reduce heat to low. Simmer 8-10 minutes or until fish is firm to the touch. Remove fish and cool.

For filling, melt 2 tablespoons butter in heavy skillet on high. Add mushrooms; reduce heat to moderate; cook 3-5 minutes, stirring occasionally until mushrooms are soft. Remove to a bowl with slotted spoon and toss with lemon juice, ½ teaspoon salt and a few grindings of pepper.

continued on page 210

The menu at brusseau's reflects the freshness and quality of the rich Northwest bounty, with vegetables and fruits harvested from local farms and orchards, and baked goods prepared from scratch with carefully selected local ingredients and served with Grandpa Cheney's homemade jams and fruit butters. Everything at Jerilyn Brusseau's delightful spot is created to nourish not only the body, but the mind and spirit as well.

CREDIT CARDS: V, MC; WHEELCHAIR ACCESS; NON-SMOKING; BEER/WINE; NO RESERVATIONS
117 Fifth Avenue South • (206) 774-4166

Melt 4 more tablespoons of butter in skillet over high heat. Add all but 1 tablespoon of the onions. Reduce heat to moderate and cook 3-5 minutes or until onions are soft. Stir in remaining 1 teaspoon of salt and ¼ teaspoon of pepper. Add to mushrooms.

Melt remaining 2 tablespoons butter in skillet over high. Add reserved tablespoon of onion. Reduce heat to moderate and cook for 2-3 minutes until soft. Add rice and cook 2-3 minutes, stirring constantly. Pour in stock, bring to boil, and cover pan tightly. Reduce heat to low and simmer for 12 minutes or until rice is tender and fluffy. Turn off heat; stir in dill, cooked mushrooms and onions, and eggs; toss lightly. Season to taste.

To assemble, place half of brioche dough on well-floured surface. Refrigerate remaining half. Quickly roll out to a rectangle ⅜ inch thick. Trim to 12 x 18 inches. Place on a parchment lined jelly roll pan. Place a layer of spinach leaves on dough; then cover with half of rice filing. Arrange salmon over rice, breaking to fit. Add another layer of spinach and cover with remaining rice filling. Spread sour cream over top and finish with a final layer of spinach leaves.

Roll out remaining dough on well-floured surface to cover top of pie. Drape dough over rolling pin and unroll over pie. Seal edges by crimping with fingers in ½-inch pleats. Cut scraps of dough into decorative shapes and arrange over top. Paint with an egg gloss of 1 egg mixed with 2 tablespoons water. Refrigerate pie 20 minutes. Place in center of a preheated 375° oven and bake for 45-60 minutes or until golden brown. Let stand 15 minutes before serving with dollops of sour cream and fresh dill.

Serves 10.

LINDAMAN'S
DARK CHOCOLATE & WHITE CHOCOLATE FROSTINGS

For Golden Chocolate Torte Recipe (see page 206)

Dark Chocolate Frosting:

Place 4 eggs and 1 cup sugar in food processor fitted with steel blade and process until well blended. Add ½ lb. unsweetened chocolate, melted, and continue to blend. With processor running, add ½ lb. unsalted butter, 1 tablespoon at at time. Blend until very smooth. Add 1 tablespoon vanilla.

White Chocolate Frosting:

Place 4 oz. unsalted butter, softened, in mixing bowl; beat until white and creamy. Add ½ cup powdered sugar and beat until smooth. Add 2 oz. white chocolate, melted. Beat until incorporated, scraping down sides of bowl. Add 1 egg and beat until fluffy.

INDEX
BY RESTAURANT

INDEX

INDEX
BY RECIPE

INDEX

Future Publications

Recipes from Old Russia

by Patte Barham and Maria Rasputin

A fascinating collection of recipes from turn-of-the-century Russia with commentary by Maria Rasputin, daughter of Grigori Efimovich Rasputin. An introduction to the cuisine of the court of Nicholas II, the last czar of Russia.

The Cook's Handy Andy

by H. A. Turner

An authentic reproduction of this classic 1932 cookbook which offers "cooks, working in commercial or plain houses, suggestions and ways of preparing the ingredients called for, in simple, quick, wholesome styles." Over 225 recipes.

For more information write:

ROMAR BOOKS, LTD.
18002 15th Ave. NE, Suite B
Seattle, WA 98155